Succeeding with Difficult Coworkers
Revised Second Edition

Joseph E. Koob II

Revised Second Edition

All rights reserved. No part of this book may be used or reproduced in any manner whatsoever without written permission from the publisher. Printed in the United States of America.

Second Revised Edition, 2019.
Copyright © 2006 by Joseph E. Koob II

For more information visit
http://www.difficultpeople.org

A difficultpeople.org publication

ISBN: 9781696395083

The Business Trilogy
By Dr. Joseph Koob

Succeeding with Difficult Coworkers
Succeeding with Difficult Bosses
Managing Difficult Employees
Revised Second Editions

Available on-line at Amazon.com:
Kindle and Paperback Editions

Books by Dr. Koob

Business Trilogy: Dealing with Change

Difficult Situations - Dealing with Change

Honoring Work and Life: 99 Words for Leaders to Live By

Leaders Managing Change

Business Trilogy: Succeeding at Work

Dealing with Difficult Coworkers

Succeeding with Difficult Bosses

Managing Difficult Employees

Dealing with Difficult Customers

Caring for Difficult Patients:
A Guide for Nursing Professionals

Books with a Personal Focus

Understanding and Working with Difficult People

ME! A Difficult Person?

Dealing with Difficult Strangers

Difficult Spouses? Improving and Saving Your Relationship with Your Significant Other

Succeeding with Difficult Professors (and Tough Courses)

Guiding Children

A Perfect Day: Guide for a Better Life

Writer's Digest Merit Award

Best book Non-fiction Oklahoma Writers Federation

Table of Contents

Preface

Part I: Key Ideas

Chapter 1	Introduction – Dealing with Difficult People	1
Chapter 2	Labels	6
Chapter 3	Dynamics in a Limited Space	9
Chapter 4	The Difficult Coworker	13
Chapter 5	Seven Keys to Being Successful with Difficult People	19
Chapter 6	Being in Control	24
Chapter 7	Knowing Yourself	27

Part II: Dealing with Difficult Behaviors

Chapter 8	Outline of Difficult Behaviors	30
Chapter 9	Getting Past the Past	35
Chapter 10	Communications	40
Chapter 11	Communicating with Difficult Colleagues	47
Chapter 12	Controlling Behaviors	53
Chapter 13	Frustrating Behaviors – Key Ideas	57
Chapter 14	'In Your Face Behaviors" – Key Ideas	71
Chapter 15	'Not quite with it' Behaviors	81
Chapter 16	'Does anyone care?' Key Ideas	89
Chapter 17	'I am better than you' Behaviors	95
Chapter 18	Really Negative Behaviors	104
Chapter 19	'The world is out to get me' Behaviors	111
Chapter 20	'Out there,' Behaviors	114
Chapter 21	'There are laws against these,' Behaviors	117
Chapter 22	Succeeding with Really Difficult Coworkers	120
Chapter 23	Things You can do that Make a Difference	124
Chapter 24	Taking Care of You	127
Chapter 25	Stay the Course	130
Bibliographies		131

Preface

This work is a needed addition to the difficult people literature. There are a number of books available that discuss difficult people in the workplace, but do not focus specifically on coworkers. There are different dynamics at work between bosses and employees, employees and their peers, and employees with their bosses. In this book I have narrowed the emphasis to helping people solve the difficulties they have at work with someone who is relatively speaking a 'coworker,' or 'colleague.' In other words, someone whose 'rank' or 'job' is roughly on the same level as theirs. [*Succeeding with Difficult Bosses* and *Managing Difficult Employees* by Dr. Joseph Koob also available at Amazon.com]

You have very likely had numerous occasions at work where someone has 'gotten on your nerves,' and if we really think about it, we have all gotten on someone else's nerves a time or two, also. Unfortunately, we all probably have had the experience of working closely with someone who just seems to get on our nerves **frequently** and the nerves of everyone else in the office or on our team.

'Difficult people' or a 'difficult person' is a bit of a misnomer. A person with a really difficult personality, i.e. someone who has a hard time relating on any kind of congenial and collegial level with you and/or other coworkers, is affecting you through their behavior. We are all still human beings. We all have our good points and bad points, our successes and failures. We all can get grumpy occasionally, or have a bad day, or react in a way that upsets another person. However, when we picture a 'difficult person', we tend to think of someone whose behavior is more consistently and pervasively negative to us and others. 'Difficulty' is a matter of degree. It is a matter of someone's behavior; It is not the whole person.

As you go through this book, we encourage you to think carefully and specifically about the types and degree of the behaviors that concern you about someone else. The more you can delineate the concerns you are having with another person at work, the easier it will be for you to find strategies that will help you learn to work with them in a successful way – a way that reduces (or eliminates) significantly the angst and problems you have had with them in the past.

This book will be divided into two major sections: **Part I** will deal with Key Ideas about working and being successful with difficult people. **Part II** will focus on applying the general ideas discussed in Part I, as well as specific strategies and tools for dealing successfully with difficult coworkers.

Please note that this work builds from one chapter to another. Many of the ideas presented in one chapter may have relevance to the next, and so on. This is also true in the chapters that deal with specific types of difficult behaviors. While it may be tempting to skip to a behavior that you want to learn to deal with, I would recommend reading through the entire book before returning to a specific chapter for additional consideration.

I also encourage you to consider reading my books, *Understanding and Working with Difficult People*, a comprehensive general approach to difficult people; and *Me! A Difficult Person?* which has a 'test' or 'scale' that helps look more closely at the types of behaviors that tend to create angst between people. Both these books provide a foundation upon which to build your skills in working with difficult people.

Addendum

Working with difficult people can be emotionally draining and even physically taxing. It may be advisable to make sure you are in good physical and emotional health as you set out on your path to success. See Chapter 29, *Taking Care of You*, for specific recommendations. [This is a chapter you can read 'out-of-order.']

Thanks

My thanks to all the usual suspects: Heath Potter, design specialist and webmaster; my good friend and editor Anne Duston, who has helped me with drafts from the beginning of difficultpeople.org, and Lisa, and Nathan, who have helped with drafts and with their support. As well as the difficult coworkers I have had the fortune to work with throughout my career. YOU have taught me a great deal!

Part I

Key Ideas

In this first section of the book we will cover some of the ideas that serve as a foundation for <u>Understanding</u> and being <u>Successful</u> with difficult people. The first chapter will Introduce key ideas from my other writings, most notably *Understanding and Working with Difficult People*, and *Me! A Difficult Person*. If you would like to consider these **Key Ideas** in more depth peruse these two important works in the difficultpeople.org literature. Chapter 2 will discuss the importance of focusing on **Behaviors** rather than using convenient labels in thinking about and ultimately dealing with people we have concerns with at work. In Chapter 3 we will talk about the **dynamics** of working in close proximity to other people in the work place and how our work situation can exacerbate difficult relationships. Chapter 4 will discuss Key Ideas that relate specifically to **working with colleagues**. In Chapter 5 we will discuss **The Seven Keys to Being Successful with Difficult People**." These are seven areas which we have found are critical to being able to be successful with people in a wide range of difficult situations.

Chapter 1

Dealing with Difficult People

Definition

At difficultpeople.org we define a difficult person as "anyone who causes anyone else angst (distress, anxiety, unease, turmoil, disquiet, tumult, upset, agitation, perturbation)."

Therefore: **we are all difficult at times**.

There are as many <u>types</u> of difficult people
as there are difficult people

This is why it is so important to focus on a person's behaviors, i.e. very specifically what they do that frustrates/irritates you (and others). We are all different and to be successful in working with others it helps tremendously to make an effort to understand them, their motivations, their foibles, and, yes, their good points, too. Sometimes just the effort we make in understanding who they are is enough to change the dynamics of our relationship with them to a more positive light.

You can only change yourself;
you cannot change other people...directly.

We don't want anyone, even someone we are very close to and care a lot about, to tell us how we should be or how we should live our life. (Ask any couple!) We especially don't want a know-it all colleague to do this. So, if you have any thoughts about changing a difficult person's way of interacting with the world by telling them what is wrong with them, you better shift gears.

The only way you can change a difficult person's behavior toward you is to change your own behavior as you interact with them.

Think about this for a minute because this is crucial to your success and to understanding everything that follows in this book.

The only way you can change a difficult person's behavior

IS

to change your own behavior.

You are probably reading this book because everything you have tried with this person in the past hasn't worked. Guess what? It ain't going to work in the future either. Plan on making some personal changes in how you approach this person, because It is the only way you will get to where you want to be: in-control, calm, and successful.

Most difficult people do not know they are being difficult.

This is one of my favorite statements because it is so hard to accept and understand. It took me a long time to realize that even the most obnoxious, controlling, rude, difficult person I ever worked with did not have a clue about how he came across to me and to others. His behavior was so outrageous that almost everyone I talked with used the big "A" word to describe him, including the VPs and the CEO of the organization.

We don't see ourselves as others see us.

And that may go triple for really difficult people.

Sandra Crowe in *Since Strangling isn't an Option* takes this a step further:

"Difficult People are generally unaware of how they affect others."

We feel as if they could care less about how they affect us, but often the truth is they really don't see how upset their behavior has made you. Yes, there are REALLY difficult people who don't care if they've upset you, and there are a few who seem to get a charge out of upsetting others. Luckily, they are few and far between. We will address these severe behavior concerns near the end of the book.

Finding out what the difficult person <u>wants, needs, or cares about</u> is KEY to understanding and working successfully with them.

The more understanding we bring to our relationships with other people, the better our chances of being successful in our dealings/work with them. Sometimes our attention and understanding are all that is needed to change the dynamics of a difficult relationship. Don't expect them to necessarily reciprocate, just make the effort. You will learn a great deal about them and about yourself in the process and you will make a huge difference in the overall relationship.

You may just find out that this person has some very admirable qualities. Sometimes it takes a good bit of patience and perseverance to get to this point. It is worth the effort!

The difficult person is getting a reward for his/her behavior.

We have learned to deal with the world and other people throughout our entire lifetime. Our behaviors, difficult or otherwise, are often the result of learned patterns that got us what we wanted or needed at some point in our life, e.g. a ranting colleague probably learned that when he got upset and started yelling, people paid attention and he got what he wanted. (These types of behaviors often have their roots in childhood.)

If it still works, why change?

Sometimes it is hard to pinpoint what a person could possibly gain from their 'impossible' behavior, but It is there. **Take away their reward** (when they deal with you) **and you take away the reason for the behavior to continue.** Keep this important point in mind throughout this book. A ranting colleague's reward might be to see you get mad, or it might be to see you cower and run crying to the bathroom, or to cave in on some point. In any case, they may feel more powerful, 'in-control,' and better about themselves as a result of your reaction.

Reaction versus Response

When we are with a person who tends to really get to us, i.e. 'pushes our buttons,' we tend to react based on our past experiences with them (and based on our past relationships and reactions to difficulties with others). One of the keys to being successful with difficult people in our lives is to gain-control of our typical **reactions** and to get a point where we can choose our **responses.**

The best way to do this is to **pay close attention** to the situation from the get go:

> Stop that need to react and step back in your mind instantaneously and observe your feelings and thoughts.
>
> Take a second to examine what those feelings and thoughts are telling you.
>
> Take another instant to consider what your 'normal' reaction would be to this negative behavior, and then consider what other more **'in-control' responses** you could make.

When we change our behavior, i.e. our **reactions**, to more in-control **responses**, we have changed the dynamics of the relationship and hence have the potential and power to change the whole relationship for the better. [See Chapter 5, *Catch It, Check It, Change It* for an in-depth discussion of this technique.]

It does boil down to choices WE make, **regardless** of their behavior to us.

Negativity breeds negativity; positivity breeds positivity

This is one of our favorite 'sayings' at difficult people.org. Our sweatshirts and tees add the suggestion: "Choose Wisely."

Another way I like to think of this is,

Negativity never helps.

It just doesn't. Think about it!

And a great perspective that takes this a step further:

Every time you are with another person, difficult or not, you have the opportunity to leave them with a negative feeling or a positive feeling. Choose kindly. Choose wisely!

Key Point:

Their behavior is not relevant.

Positivity should be your choice, always.

> Accept responsibility for the choices you make. (Perkins/Koob)

Being Right versus being Kind

We humans invest a tremendous amount of energy (often negative energy) in 'being right.' A while back at a seminar a person asked me if there was a way to be right and be kind at the same time. My answer was, "Yes, we can always find ways to be kind." Later that evening, I thought about this a long time and realized I had only partially answered the question. I should have also asked a question in return, "What is so all-fired important about being right?"

Think about this statement: 95% of the time (or more) the only reason we need **to be right** is because our **ego** is demanding it of us.

The next time you are having a difficult experience with a 'difficult person,' ask yourself whether you and they are both trying **to be right** and what you will actually (be honest) lose if you give up 'being right.' When you realize you are not really giving up anything except ego, **choose 'being kind' instead.**

Important: You don't have to be wrong either. Most of the time, being right has to do with stubbornness on TWO people's parts. When one stops 'being right' (hint: It is not likely going to be your difficult colleague), there are often ways to find other, mutually acceptable solutions to the issues at hand.

You can learn a tremendous amount from difficult people.

Why is this REALLY difficult person in your life?

I can't answer that question, but you might be able to if you take the perspective that life is trying to teach you something. Perhaps this angel, in the disguise of a not so angelic character, IS there to teach you something. Open your eyes, mind, and heart -- you might learn a tremendous amount about yourself and others by changing your outlook slightly -- by trying to understand as much as possible from your interactions and relationships with this difficult person.

If you are successful in dealing with this difficult person/situation, you will have learned a great deal about how to be successful with future similar experiences and other similar difficult people.

Another perspective I have held for a long time is: I can always learn how NOT to behave, act, interact from the difficult people in my life. Amazingly enough, I don't have anywhere nearly as many difficult people in my life anymore – curious...

People are different – It is the most common cause for angst between people

Often, we have difficulties with other people because we don't see eye-to-eye. Differences between people ARE the most common reason people don't get along. When we can open our minds and learn to accept that others see and interpret the world differently from us (often very differently), we can understand how difficulties can arise and learn to work/coexist together in spite of them.

Change Takes Time

To be successful with difficult people you need to change how you interact with them. It does take understanding – why you are reading this book – effort, and time. We have developed ingrained habits in how we relate and work with others. To change those, you need to not only look at relationships and interactions differently, you have to learn to take that understanding and use it to develop your own personal tools and skills for making a difference in your interactions with difficult others.

If you are dealing with a colleague who you have a long history with, it may take even a bit more understanding and effort. It is hard to erase the past.

The Best News Yet

It is possible! And you CAN do it. Stay the course and work/practice with the understandings and skills you learn. Read as much as you can and try to apply your new understandings and skills in all your relationships with others. Hopefully, you will soon wonder where all those difficulties went.

Questions and Ideas for Contemplation

Take a few moments with each of the highlighted ideas above and see how they affect the way you consider the difficult person you are concerned with at work. If something strikes you as particularly significant, make a note of it and keep it handy as you read through the rest of the book.

Many of the ideas in this first chapter will be expanded upon in a variety of ways throughout this text. Be sure to revisit this chapter occasionally to see how your understanding has changed.

Chapter 2
Labels

One of the interesting traits of humanity is our almost obsessive need to organize things. Even the most liberal and free-spirited of us uses organization as a tool. The more perfectionist sorts go to great lengths to set things in 'proper' order or to determine an order for things that don't necessarily have an order. We get upset if we can't explain things or if something just doesn't make sense. We organize everything from our roads to our houses to our understanding of the universe. Sometimes it works and sometimes... well, let's just say other things get in the way.

We also tend to categorize and label people, unfortunately so. I have read most of the currently available literature on difficult people and it always interests me when an author uses a name or label as a means of organizing and explaining the behaviors of 'difficult people.' Here are a few examples: Tank, Exploder, Sniper, Busybody, Hostile Ape, Sarcastic Bee, Prickly Porcupine, Know-it-all-Owl, and so on. [See the Bibliography for a list of works from the **Difficult People Literature.**]

The advantage of this type of labeling is that it immediately gives us an image we can latch on to of what this person is like. It also allows us to categorize people into neat little groups so we can discuss this 'type' as a whole. The disadvantage is that no one ever fits conveniently or completely into these neat 'types.' **We are all different** and we all approach other people in our own unique and difficult (if such is the case) way.

From long personal experience and study, every difficult person I have known, discussed with clients, or read about, has a variety of difficult patterns of behavior and they don't fit into any neat category or typing. In addition, it is VERY common for a person who exhibits one difficult behavior, e.g. putting people down on a regular basis, to switch to another behavior when this behavior is challenged or doesn't get them what they want, e.g. if putting you down to your face doesn't work anymore, they may try to sabotage you behind your back.

You cannot typecast personalities

Please don't try!

It can cause much more harm than good, unless used by trained professionals in a professional clinical setting.

One of the books I read in preparation for writing this book was **Toxic Coworkers: How to Deal with Dysfunctional People on the Job.** It is a psychiatrically/psychologically-based book that uses the **Diagnostic and Statistical Manual of Mental Disorders,** Fourth Edition (DSM-IV) of the American Psychiatric Association as a jumping off source to discuss "Personality Disorders." There is a great deal of interesting and valuable information offered in this book; but please be aware that diagnosing, i.e. labeling, a person with a personality disorder should only be done by a qualified professional.

I have had courses on and about Abnormal Psychology, and studied and worked with the **DSM-IV**. I have the **DSM-IV** sitting on my shelf. I have used it for preliminary diagnoses when working with a qualified psychologist as a mentor during my internship and later as a counselor. Still, I do not consider myself qualified to look at a person's behavior patterns and label them with a personality disorder. I would need further training and more direct experience working with a psychologist or psychiatrist. As a personal and executive coach, I would never use this kind of labeling in my work with difficult people or with people who are having concerns with difficult people.

In one sense, we all exhibit mild forms of a wide variety of the symptoms associated with personality disorders. For example: at times we all are slightly paranoid (fearful, think someone is doing/working something behind our backs, etc.) It is very important to understand that the DSM-IV is merely a guide to the types of symptoms that are common to a particular personality disorder and the criteria for any given disorder are typically:

> that the symptoms are 'pervasive'
>
> that they have been exhibited for some time
>
> and that the person exhibits 'x' number of symptoms from a given list.

There is a great deal of flexibility built in for the experienced professional to make intelligent decisions relevant to a specific person. The manual is meant for use by qualified professionals in a clinical situation and for, in my opinion, to be used ONLY by qualified professionals in discussing and working with these issues **with** another professional in order to help a patient.

A little knowledge can be a dangerous thing

Not only can this type of type-casting cause serious concerns if used by unqualified people, it could also set you up for litigious action. NEVER label a person with a 'label,' 'name,' or 'designation' you are not professionally qualified to make. You may think a person has some specific concern, but such labeling serves no purpose what-so-ever in helping you deal with difficult behaviors!

Understand the Behavior

Discuss behaviors, don't typecast

In this book we will discuss a wide range of **behaviors** that can and do irritate other people. It is the behavior of a person who causes us considerable angst that we need to resolve with them and with ourselves. I personally don't feel it does anyone any good, you or your 'difficult person' to label them in any way (including labeling them "difficult"). When we focus on behaviors, very specific behaviors, that bother us, we have something we can deal with.

At the beginning of Part II of this book we will provide a list of behaviors that may cause difficulties between two people. We will also suggest several ways for you to understand the different aspects of a person's character and behavior that bother you on a regular basis. When you do this type of exercise you can begin to see the **patterns of behaviors** that typically concern you. In the process you will learn a good bit about yourself, about the specific person you are concerned with, and most likely about other people who have caused you similar concerns in the past.

When we discuss specific 'categories' of difficult behaviors later in this book please remember that the purpose in organizing behaviors together is for the ease of discussion. These groupings are not meant to be used as labels.

If you need to organize...

It is very helpful to set out in great detail the characteristics of a troublesome person's behavior in order to focus on what you need to do to be successful with them. It is an excellent personal exercise to work on (see Part II, Chapter 7 for several exercises we recommend). However, please don't share this information with others as a statement of fact. If you are working with a coach or counselor you certainly could discuss it with them as there is a code of confidentiality, and if you have a very close and trusted friend, you might want to run some ideas past them. Just try to avoid labels. Very few people are always one way or another.

Look for the good things, too

I have worked with, mentored, and helped hundreds of people in my life. One essential truth is that we all have good traits and we all have more 'difficult' things about our personalities, too... especially if you consider that we all look at things a bit differently from each other and **differences** tend to cause angst between people. It takes a positive, in-control person to look beyond the difficult and find the good when working with a very negative, 'difficult' person, but it can pay huge benefits.

When we look for the good in others, we will find it. And surprisingly, when we look, and the more we look, the more they will be willing to show it to us, and the more the difficulties will fade away.

Questions and Ideas for Contemplation

Consider the images that come to your mind when you think about a difficult person in your life. How would you describe them? How HAVE you described them in the past (to yourself, to others)? How broad and general are these perceptions and observations? Do you think in terms of, "Boy is he a/an___" or do you try to focus in on the actual behaviors that cause them to be a certain way?"

In Part II, Chapter 7 we will come back to the issue of identifying the behaviors that bother you about a given difficult person in your life. Then in Chapter 8 we will introduce some specific ideas and exercises for working though some of your angst and frustrations with past difficult personalities you have had to deal with. Keep this in mind: knowledge, very specific knowledge, can help increase your personal power and confidence in being successful with difficult people and difficult situations.

Chapter 3

The Office
Dynamics in Limited Space

The relationships we have at our place of work are partially defined by the layout, conditions, and dynamics of the space and culture we are in. Many times, we do not have a choice, or much of a choice, in working with these constraints. However, it is worth the time and effort to consider how these restrictions may impact the difficulties you are having with another person.

It is a System

Every work space and culture is different, but they all have something in common, everything works off of everything else – there is a system, for better or for worse, that in different ways drives the relationships of the people in it.

A work system is often not unlike a family system. How one person impacts the system affects all the relationships close to that person in the system. In a family the parents and children all interact to uphold the status quo of the current family system, good or bad. Even the grandparents and other relatives can have an impact on the family and how it interacts. The set-up or culture of the family system has a long history and much of the dynamics within a family group have come down through both sides of the family for many, many years. There is a balance, whether it works well or not, that has become an accepted way of doing things in the system and when someone tries to change that, the rest of the system reacts to re-balance itself.

Work is the same in many ways. Employees, Directors, Senior Directors, VPs, even the support staff, all affect the way the system works. When something (someone) is not working well in the system it impacts everyone. And here's the really important point – **everyone has**, in some way, **an impact on what continues in the system**, good or bad.

The key to being successful with a specific difficult colleague at work is that you are not just working to solve your concerns with them, but working to change, in effect, the dynamics of their relationship with you. This will not only affect both of you, but the rest of the system as well. That type of change takes time, perseverance, and courage.

Colleagues

In this book we are focusing on relationships at work that are more or less equal. However, keep in mind that you may also have to consider how what you do will impact employees under you and bosses above you, as well as other colleagues on your team and across the matrices.

Stay alert to the dynamics of relationships as you change yourself (the only way you will effect change in your difficult person). Stay open and honest about what is important to you; and be willing to talk to others who may be impacted by your new approach to this individual, to everyone in general, and to your work. You will change if you do this self-help work; and as a result, all of your relationships at work will be impacted, not just the one you are concerned with.

Cliques and other Intrigues

Offices are often hotbeds for all types of intrigue, gossip, and various other groups. Difficult people tend to be a big part of the mix of what is happening in any given work space. You can choose to be part of this type of stuff, or you can choose to be yourself and not be draw into or influenced by negativity that is being perpetrated and spread through devious means.

People understand very quickly who you are, what you are about, and what is important to you if you let them know assertively and kindly. While it often takes time, good people will recognize positive self-worth and quality hard work. Eventually a truly consistent positive force in any group can have a remarkable effect. Negativity will find itself off in a corner being ignored. [Hint: Negative people WILL try to re-balance the system by finding other ways to be influential.]

Stick to your guns -- your positive, self-confident self! (See Chapter 5, *The Seven Keys to Understanding and Working with Difficult People*) If you do, over the long run they will finally get the idea that you and others would much rather take a more positive path. It takes patience and courage on your part, but it does work.

Spaces

Today's work spaces are often less than ideal. Cubicles, wide open spaces, and other office layouts have advantages and disadvantages. Space relationships can exacerbate interpersonal difficulties: too many people in too few spaces; limited space; isolation; no privacy; big versus small spaces, coupled with seniority and other issues, and so on.

How your work space is maintained can also be a major source of frustration: cleanliness (including restrooms and other facilities), decor, modernization, technological access, etc.

Turf wars are not uncommon. Sometimes a difficult relationship with a colleague may be something as simple as how they feel about their "space," in relationship to yours or others.

Paying attention to these details and making the effort to understand them and how they impact you and others can help ease tensions. It may not solve the current problem, but getting it out in the open and discussing these issues can make a big difference. People like to be heard, under-stood, and appreciated – and importantly, they don't always have to be right when these key elements are present.

This is another VERY important point worth highlighting:

People like to be heard, understood, and appreciated.

They don't always have to be right if these are present.

People will notice

If you change the way you interact with a person or persons at work, people will notice. They will notice changes you make in how you feel, how you carry yourself, and how you interact with others. If one person notices or knows something, be assured that soon everyone will know.

One of the sure dynamics of limited space is that nothing is ever confidential. That can be excellent when you are making positive changes and having a positive impact at work, but a word of caution is advised. Keep in mind that if you choose to discuss concerns you have, problems you see, and so on, that it is highly likely, even if you are talking with a trusted friend, that it will eventually get around.

It pays to be a little cautious, but don't get paranoid either. **Being open and honest is a big key to being successful with difficult people,** but **being kind, compassionate, and avoiding negativity at the same time goes hand-in-hand.**

People might feel threatened

Bosses, colleagues, coworkers can feel threatened by the new you. Even if all the changes you are making are completely positive (and hopefully they are), people could see the new assertive, positive you as somehow jeopardizing the 'status quo.' Remember people are used to the way things were and people often dislike change.

Keep on course and don't get discouraged. Your positive change will ultimately effect positive change around you. It does work! Persevere!

If you see someone as difficult,

it is very likely that they see you as being difficult.

This is another key idea about understanding difficult people. 'Difficulty' is rarely a one-way street. Yes, the person you are concerned with may be a complete jerk and someone who treats everyone badly; however, they still might (will, very likely) see you (and others) as being the difficult one(s). It is often about how differently we, and they, perceive the world.

Keep this important point in mind as part of the overall dynamics of your workspace. Interactions flow in many directions, and in many, often hard to believe, ways.

Stay in touch with your boss(es)

You can even let her/him know what you are trying to accomplish. Just be sure you know, and they know, that you are working to improve yourself and your work. They may get a mixed message from the changes you make and from other colleagues who are 'concerned' or 'involved.' For example:

> It is not unusual for a difficult colleague to seek a different outlet, e.g. to complain, whine, etc. to someone else or the boss, if you are no longer their punching bag.
>
> Guess who they will whine and complain about?

Consider the culture of your organization

Most corporations have a specifically delineated culture, i.e. values, qualities, a mission that everyone is supposed to aspire to, etc. Organizations, groups, and teams also often have an unspoken credo of how things should be done, as well as how they always have been done. Try to keep these concepts in mind as you make personal changes. Everything you will be working on related to this book will be positive self-work. Keeping the formal and informal aspects of your organization and team(s) in mind as you effect change is smart politics and it helps make everything transition more smoothly.

It is all about paying attention

Working with a difficult person and the behaviors that really frustrate us tends to be a very narrow focus. Just keep in mind that there are many others who will be impacted by changes you make and things you do. Keeping a positive handle on how they are being affected makes good sense and keeps you in tune with all the dynamics of your work space. This way your impact will be a positive force throughout.

Questions and Ideas for Contemplation

What dynamics at work might have an impact on changes you wish to make? How might people will be affected if you succeed in changing your relationship with this difficult person for the better? Can you envision what your team, matrix, work relationships will be like if you succeed with your difficult person?

These are all good questions to consider as you develop the understanding and skills to make the changes you want to make with this relationship at work.

Chapter 4

The Difficult Coworker

Our Colleagues

The people we work with are not necessarily our pick for life companions; but we all have a basic choice to make in a work situation: we succeed in having a decent, if not enjoyable working relationship, or we don't succeed and there are concerns with one or more people we work closely with. If we don't succeed, and have major concerns on a regular basis with someone; then we can choose to change how we interact and react to this person, or we can leave and hope our next position has more amenable people. [Hint: I have yet to work at a business, except for working for myself, that didn't have difficult people concerns.]

The difficult thing to accept sometimes is that the choices rest firmly on OUR shoulders. We can blame others, complain to whoever will listen that the person we have to deal with is IMPOSSIBLE, and fight a consistently losing battle with them; but, unless we are willing to accept responsibility to make a difference, **no amount of complaining, blaming, or excuses will make a difference**.

Negativity breeds negativity – make more positive choices. That is what the rest of this book is about.

Keep in mind that you are a colleague and an equal. Don't assume a role that is inappropriate, i.e. acting in a supervisory capacity, mentor, etc. It can get you in trouble. You can take on other roles IF a colleague brings it up first and/or asks you for help. Trust is a major issue in changing and developing a positive working relationship with a person who has been causing you considerable angst.

Control

Probably the most important issue in difficult people interactions is the 'fight' for control. We all want to be in-control. With difficult people it is almost a matter of life and death.

Difficult people try to control others and situations through several means, including: intimidation (outbursts, domineering behaviors, nit-picking, etc.), by manipulation (going behind your back, cheating. Lying, etc.), and with childish behaviors (whining, complaining, withdrawing, etc.) that have been effective for them throughout their lives. Unfortunately, we often buy into these behaviors by **reacting** the way they want us to.

A colleague or coworker may try to apply leverage (seniority, power, 'I am IN with the boss, etc.) to control you, but in most work situations ranks and levels are very specifically delineated. If they do not have formal authority over you, then you have the right to stand up for yourself in an assertive and positive way as an equal. [Dealing with a difficult person who does have formal authority over you is another whole ball game and is not specifically addressed in this book. Many of the techniques you will learn in this book CAN be applied in any difficult person situation. Just keep in mind that the dynamics of the situation require a different approach. (See *Succeeding with Difficult Bosses*, Koob)]

Fight or Flight

We generally **react** to difficult behaviors by **fighting** (anger, fighting or yelling back, getting defensive, etc.) or by flight (withdrawing, letting them have their way, avoidance, etc.). The curious thing about our reactions is that while we 'design' them to maintain-control, the truth is, whenever we react negatively to another person's behavior, we are allowing them to control us.

This is so important that it is worth reiterating:

> When we **REACT** negatively to a difficult person's behavior (even if it is extremely negative), we are allowing them to control our choices, our emotions, our peace of mind.
>
> When we can **RESPOND** in a self-controlled, assertive, positive way, then we have not bought into their negativity and need for control.

Believe it or not this is possible in all difficult people interactions.

Don't be a victim

Often a difficult person's behavior makes us feel pretty bad, regardless of how we react.

> "Arrows only do harm when they hit a target." (Crowe)

Hint: **Stop being a target!**

I spent a fair amount of my life being a victim of difficult people. Over the course of working on myself and understanding the dynamics of interpersonal relationships, I moved from being a victim to being able to succeed with difficult people.

Here is one way to see yourself moving out of being a victim:

From being a Victim of a Difficult Person (they frustrate us, push our buttons):

> to Surviving difficult encounters with them
>
> to Coping with their difficult behavior and our reactions to it
>
> to Dealing with our reactions, emotions by making more positive choices
>
> to Winning with these situations on a daily basis
>
> to Succeeding with *Understanding and Working with the Difficult People* in your work place

With the information and skills you can learn from this book, it is my hope you can move very quickly to succeeding with difficult people. The first step is not allowing yourself to be a target any more. You always have the right and can make the choice to present a positive, assertive you to the world.

Difficult Coworkers (People) want Something

People behave the way they behave because they want something. They may not, and often don't, really understand what they want. In their book *Dealing with People You Can't Stand*, Brinkman and Kirschner have an excellent section on understanding difficult peoples' intent:

> Intent:
>> Get it Done
>>
>> Get it Right
>>
>> Get along
>>
>> Get appreciation

I have added one more to their list:

>> To be Cared for

They want something because they often:

> Feel insecure, lack confidence, don't get enough attention or recognition, don't understand themselves or others, don't want to feel inferior (but often do), are afraid (to lose, to be put-down, to be left out, to be left behind, to not succeed, etc.), feel they need to be in-control, and so on.

We will discuss intent, needs, wants, and desires more when we cover different types of difficult behaviors. A few examples, see below, offer a number of interesting perspectives:

> "**Get it done**" people often have difficulties with "**Get it right**" people, and vice versa.

> For example: A really perfectionist type may spend a great deal of time getting things just right to the utter consternation of the coworker who wants to get this project off the table and move ahead. Both these people would likely irritate each other, and over time resentments could very well escalate to very serious interpersonal and work concerns.

> A person who **needs to be appreciated** for what they do could be very frustrated with a colleague whose over-all manner is close-mouthed, efficient, and focuses only on their own issues.

> A person who **needs to get along with others** can be deeply affected and offended by an aloof, unsentimental coworker, who avoids all social contact and rarely communicates except for required business-related snippets.

> A person who **needs to be cared for** may feel rejected by coworkers who ignore their needs, wants, and desires and who make no effort to 'bring them into the fold.'

> And so on.

Keep these broad ideas in mind as we cover various behavior patterns and you will see how much our needs affect our interpersonal relationships at work. Acknowledgment, appreciation, recognition, feeling that someone at work cares about us and how we are doing, our need to get things done or get things right, etc. all impact how we get along with others. Sometimes easing difficulties in relationships is a 'simple' matter of paying attention to our own needs and to the needs of the people we have concerns with. This understanding can make a huge difference in how we approach and work with our colleagues.

It is important to emphasize that **knowing our own needs, wants, desires, and general intent** can also be a very eye-opening experience. Observe yourself the next time you are with a person you have had difficulties with and try to figure out what is motivating you and what is driving your concerns. It can be very surprising to discover the types of things that affect us very dramatically in a relationship.

What do they want?

When you have to deal with a difficult person on a regular basis, try this the next time you work closely with them: ask yourself, "What do they want?" Hint: it is often, very often, not the thing the person is ranting about. It typically goes much deeper than that.

When we can better understand a person's wants, needs, desires, and their intent, we have made a major leap in being able to succeed in developing a collegial working relationship with them.

Just the effort we make in trying to better understand a person we have had a difficult past with changes the dynamics of our interactions with them. As we develop the skills to understand, and to fulfill some of their needs, the relationship can change dramatically.

No, it isn't your job or responsibility to fulfill another person's wants, needs, or desires at work, and it may be the farthest thing from your mind when putting up with difficult behavior. However, if it can make a significant difference in your own survival and enjoyment at work, isn't it worth a little bit of effort?

Difficult people can be very needy

Difficult people can be very difficult because they have tremendous needs. A real perfectionist-type may never be satisfied with the quality of work you or others do. A person who never got the appreciation and recognition they needed and deserved when growing up may need all the support and encouragement they can get. And so on. You can't change their past, and you can't change who they are and their deep-rooted needs. **You can make a difference in your relationship with them** by doing what you can for them while maintaining your own self-control and self-worth.

Little efforts can make major differences!

Difficult people want to be understood

You can:

Make an effort to understand them (which is often appreciated)

Really listen to them (without judgement is key)

Pay attention to them and try to understand what they want

Make an effort to do what you can do within the scope of who you are and what is important to you, to help with their needs, wants, desires, and intent.

Difficult people become even more difficult when they are misunderstood (or perceive to be misunderstood) or ignored.

(Bell and Smith, and Koob)

And this is even more obvious and intense with really difficult people.

It seems like it would be so simple a thing to **make the effort** to understand another person; unfortunately, we often let our 'stuff' get in the way. A very useful technique in working successfully with difficult personalities is to really learn **to pay attention and listen** so that we better understand who they are, where they are coming from, and what they want. It makes all the difference in the world!

> For example: Think about your last bad or so-so interaction with a customer service representative and contrast that with a good interaction. Chances are the good rep. made an effort to help you feel like they wanted to understand what was important to you. The other reps, 'Could have cared less' and you probably felt like they just wanted to get through another call.

"The one who understands guides or controls." (Crowe)

The more you understand another person and what motivates them, the better in-control you can be of your own responses and feelings, and the less likely you will give over control to them by reacting negatively. It is important to realize that the purpose of understanding another person is not a means for you to raise yourself above them or to control them, that is ego at work; but to allow yourself the freedom to maintain-control of yourself, and to help them understand who you are and what is important to you. As you will see in the next chapter, our ultimate aim is self-control, not control of others.

"Suggest new behaviors or options." (Brinkman and Kirschner)

When push comes to shove, it is always appropriate for you to stand up for yourself kindly. If an over-the-top colleague is always yelling at you, you may need to tell them as compassionately as possible that their behavior bothers you and that you would appreciate a more controlled approach.

> "Bill, you always come to me with excellent ideas and concerns; however, I need you to understand that when you yell at me, I get very upset. Would it be possible for us to find a way to be collegial in all our interactions? It would make all the difference for me. Thanks."

Another great way to look at this comes from Feldner's book, *Does Someone at Work Treat you Badly?*

> **"Teach them how you want to be treated."**

There are always positive ways we can show others how we wish to be treated.

Questions and Ideas for Contemplation

The above discussion focuses on some very fundamental issues we need to understand to be successful in dealing with difficult people. It is easy to blame things on them, and they probably deserve the blame; but it is very important to understand that until we accept responsibility for changing ourselves, so that we ultimately change the situation for the better, **all forms of negativity won't help – no matter who's to blame.**

Choose now to stop being a victim and to make an effort to change how you approach the difficult person (people) in your life. Keep this important thought in mind throughout the rest of this book:

> **What you have done in the past hasn't worked!**
>
> **You need to do some things differently to succeed.**

Chapter 5

The Seven Keys to Being Successful with Difficult People

Working successfully with other people centers around how we feel about ourselves. Their 'stuff' has a direct effect on **how they interact with us** but doesn't have to affect how we feel or go about our own work. When we can step beyond their problems and live our life to the fullest, and make the most of our work on OUR terms, we have learned to truly be in-control.

The Seven Keys to being Successful with Difficult People came about through the ongoing development of literature available at difficultpeople.org – a web site dedicated to *Understanding and Working with Difficult People*. As you work on your strengths in these important areas you will notice a marked difference and improvement in how you perceive 'difficult' people you work with and how you handle their difficult interpersonal behaviors.

These *Seven Keys* are all centered in your attitude about yourself and others:

Self-awareness

Self-worth

Self-Confidence

Self-Control

Honesty

Kindness

Positivity

Self-awareness

We all would like to think we know ourselves pretty well. The truth is, we probably don't. We tend not to pay very much attention to much of what impacts us during the day, how we react to it, how we feel about it, and how it affects us (especially in the long run). **Self-awareness is about PAYING ATTENTION** to all of these things. The more we are on top of our interactions with others, the easier it is for us to understand and deal with concerns that arise. Our feelings and reactions are critical to how we deal with other people successfully, particularly difficult people who enter our lives.

Self-awareness tops this list because it is fundamental to all the other ideas. When we begin to understand ourselves better, we can make better choices, and we build our self-worth, self-confidence, and self-control. **There is no better tool available for you to help build your foundation for dealing effectively and positively with others.**

How to?

Working on your ability to **pay attention** or **self-observe** takes practice and patience. You want it to become a positive habit that helps you in your interactions with others.

The basics are:

> Practice taking a step back in your mind whenever you start to feel upset frustrated, uncomfortable.
>
> Observe very specifically what you are feeling and thinking.
>
> Observe how you normally would react to this frustration.

Finally: you now have the control to make a different, more positive choice for yourself.

You can train yourself to do this whole process almost instantaneously. [See next Chapter, *Being in-control* for an excerpt from *Understanding and Working with Difficult People* that discusses this technique in a in more detail.]

Working on your self-awareness pays big dividends.

Self-worth

> It is your self-worth. "Don't let anyone else define it."
>
> (Axelrod and Holtje)

Self-worth is how we value ourselves. It has nothing to do with ego, i.e. placing ourselves above others. It has to do with who we truly believe we are and how we bring that to the world. It has to do with understanding our most fundamental values, i.e. the person we would most like to be.

There are several ways to look at this, but it all comes back to knowing who we are (who we want to be) through self-awareness, and bringing that to the fore. Here are two ways I get my clients to consider this critical concept:

> Ask yourself what **values/qualities** you would like to instill in your children as they grow up. What are the most fundamental truths you would like them to have as they begin their own independent life? [See Chapter 7, *Knowing Yourself*, for an excerpt from my book, *Guiding Difficult Children*, that presents the exercise in detail.]

Another way to look at this is to ask yourself this question:

> How do I want others to perceive my life and work after I am gone?

In other words, what kind of legacy do you really want to leave. (You have to think hard about this, to have it be effective.)

Self-confidence

As we develop our self-worth, our self-confidence improves. We can work on our confidence by working on our self-awareness at every opportunity. Many of the difficulties we have with other people are affected a great deal by our inability to maintain a confident and positive demeanor when we are with them. You can be assured that if you are getting upset, defensive, depressed, etc. that your confidence is taking a hit.

Assertiveness is being able to accept yourself in an interaction with another person regardless of their behavior. It does take practice and self-awareness. If you feel you could use some help in this area please work with a coach or take a seminar on assertiveness. These can help you tremendously in learning how to stand-up for yourself positively in difficult situations.

Self-control

As mentioned in Chapter 4, **Control is a major issue in difficult interactions.** Control of other people is an illusion. It is an illusion that drives difficult people to their difficult behaviors. When they do 'X' they feel more in-control of their world. To be successful with difficult people our only recourse is **self-control. We are not out to control them; only our own feelings, thoughts, and responses to their difficult behaviors.** When we are in-control, they almost always don't have any choice but to change their negative behavior when interacting with us.

We see other people as difficult because we often (most often) turn control over to them. A ranting, exploding colleague only is effective if we get angry, or cower, or react in some negative way. If we stand our ground in a relaxed and positive way, they are eventually going to see that their behavior isn't having any affect on us. Bingo! We have succeeded in maintaining our control, our self-worth, and changing their negative interactions with us.

No one can control our lives without our permission! We always have positive choices we can make. Sometimes they are difficult to understand or to see. Practice in self-awareness, awareness and understanding of others, and in developing our self-worth and self-confidence can make all the difference.

Honesty

This one seems pretty basic, but honesty means being honest with ourselves (more self-awareness!) and being kindly honest with others:

> "John, I appreciate everything you are saying. It all makes good sense, but I would appreciate it if in the future we could have an in-depth discussion without you becoming so upset."

> "Alice, I don't know if this is true; however, I want you to know that I have heard from several sources that you are spreading rumors about me around the team. Please come to me if you have any concerns. I am more than willing to work with you on anything that is bothering you. I would like to have a collegial working relationship with you. We can do that if we are both willing to be open and honest with each other. Please understand that I won't tolerate negative, behind-the-back talk from anyone."

Both of these statements come from a self-aware, self-worth, self-confident, in-control, positive, and honest stance. You always have a right to be honest with others and there are ALWAYS positive ways to do that.

Kindness

Every interaction we have with other people has the opportunity for us to be kind, or to be something else. Practicing kindness, especially in the face of difficult behavior, pays huge dividends. Try it! You will be pleasantly surprised.

Hint: this can be difficult to do with people that you have a past history with, but it will work with them too, in the long run. Be patient and keep at it!

It can be really tough to be kind and compassionate in the face of a very disagreeable, inflexible person. Try to keep in mind that this difficult person is a child of the universe no less than you. Whatever 'stuff,' past and current, has them where they currently are, is perhaps quite unfortunate, for you, and especially for them. You may be able to make a positive difference to their existence, even if it is only for a short time. **And you may very well be the catalyst that helps them start to turn their life around!**

Positivity

Always keep in mind our favorite saying at difficultpeople.org:

Negativity breeds Negativity

Positivity breeds Positivity

Choose Wisely

And that pretty much says it all. **We always can choose to be positive, even in the face of negativity.** When we do make the right choice, we have the opportunity to help change someone else's day, week, maybe even their life, around. Wow!

The Seven Keys

As we discuss difficult behaviors and how we can respond to them in a more positive, successful way throughout the rest of this book, keep these seven Key Ideas in mind. You will see that they play a fundamental role in how we can successfully approach others. We will add a good bit more to them, but these really do set the foundation for your success.

Questions and Ideas for Contemplation

How would you rate yourself on each of these Seven Keys? Can you be completely honest and really assess where you might need some work? Try using a simple form like the one below and see how it comes out. Put it some place safe for a period of time; then after you have read the rest of this book, come back to this page and do this again. Are there any differences from the first time you did this?

You can do this specifically for work and/or for all of your personal interactions.

This is for you and the 'scoring' of this has no relevance to anything or anyone else. It is simply meant as a learning tool. Please do not use this with other people unless they know in advance that it is not a formal scale and as such has not been standardized, tested, or validated statistically.

Use any scale-type measure you like. Here is an example:

Fair		Needs Work		Good		Very Good		Strong
1	2	3	4	5	6	7	8	9

Then list the *Seven Keys* and score relative to how you feel about each one in how you approach people at work.

You can set this up on graph paper, or with some type of illustration/guide you devise on your computer. It can be as simple as:

Self-awareness	5
Self-worth	4
Self-Confidence	6
Self-Control	8
Honesty	8
Kindness	4
Positivity	4

Really DO try to be brutally honest, and please DO NOT share this with others. This is for your own self-work and self-knowledge.

The value is that you really can see what you feel you need to work on, and if you do this again, perhaps in three months or a year, you will hopefully see marked improvement. Working with and on these **Seven Keys** can really make a difference in your life and in your work with others.

Chapter 6

Being In-Control

Who is in-control?

Most difficult people are trying to get control of you, in a sense, of the situation. It is one of the most common characteristics of a difficult personality. Unfortunately, with their tactics, whatever they may be, they often achieve exactly what they want. They have learned to push other people's buttons as a means of controlling them and the situation

Wanting to be in-control is also a general characteristic of the human race. None of us likes to feel we are not in-control, or to feel we are being controlled by others. It is the amount of control we try to wield over others that makes the difference between someone we and others may see as difficult and, well, hopefully the rest of us.

We will discuss the difficult people side of control more in a later chapter. For now, we want to focus on YOU and what you can do to make a difference.

Being in-control

The object of paying attention to yourself is not to control others, but to be in-control of yourself. At the root, this means not giving over your emotions, your power, your behavior (reaction) to another person. It has to do with **Self-control** and **Assertiveness**.

Assertiveness is, fundamentally, **being able to stand up for yourself in a positive way.**

Staying in-control of you

Several years ago, when I was working at the VA Medical Center in San Diego, I was fortunate to work with Dr. John McQuaid. In the course of my writing several manuals for drug and alcohol group therapy, John introduced me to something he had written for use with the patients. As with many good ideas, this one is simple and easy to remember:

Catch It

Check It

Change It

While the concept isn't new, the **3 C's** makes it easy to remember.

Catch it!

The first step in gaining and maintaining self-control in a difficult situation is to **Catch** yourself. **Paying Attention equals "Catch it"**

By paying attention to your emotions, what you are thinking, and the reaction you are about to have, you set yourself up for **making a choice**, instead of **reacting,** as you might typically do in a difficult situation with a difficult person.

Choices...

...are everything in difficult situations. Rather than buying into the other person's mania or difficulty and immediately reacting, you can now be who you want to be – who you **choose** to be. You make the choices.

Check it

While this may seem like the obvious next step, it is not always so clear cut. You want everything about this difficult situation you find yourself in to be very clear for you. Checking it helps you set up making different choices than you would normally make.

Take a look at your feelings, your thoughts, and your soon to be reaction.

> **Is this really how you want to feel, think, and react?**

The bomb didn't go off?

The simple act of checking these inner workings of your mind and body does a very important thing. **It sets up a pause** in the 'proceedings.' That pause means you are still in-control and you haven't let your emotions take over. It will also, very likely, puzzle the heck out of the difficult people you are dealing with. He wants, and is waiting for, the expected reaction from you – loss of control – anger, upset, frustration, fear, etc.

Change it

You now have the choice of redirecting yourself and the situation. As you will find out, this makes all the difference in the world in dealing with difficult people.

Remember

> **Catch it** – are you paying attention to yourself?
>
> **Check it** – is this really how you want to be?
>
> **Change it** – make a different choice

While it is important to pay attention to yourself, it is important to pay attention to the person you are dealing with, too. The first part of this book is about **what you are bringing into a difficult situation**; the rest of the book **focuses on understanding what the other person is bringing to the equation.**

Here is an example of a difficult situation using *Catch it, Check it, Change it* to alter the dynamics with this particular difficult person's approach:

> You are going about your work day diligently and conscientiously as normal. You have gotten a lot done, but there see still several contracts you need to check for progress, and a new file is awaiting your attention on the side of your desk. Without preamble, a colleague walks through your partially open door into your office and starts complaining loudly

about something to do with a contract you had passed on to him over a month ago.

You are aware that at least half the office probably can hear this guy's rant, and you are desperately trying to think back about what he could possibly be upset about. You felt like you had done a good job with your part of the contract and passed it along the chain when you had completed your work.

By the time you realize he is ragging on about something that was really his responsibility, you feel backed into a corner, embarrassed, and are getting more upset by the moment.

You begin to...

How do you react?

Do you get red in the face, set your jaw, and get ready to fight back with angry words? Defending yourself against his attack.

OR, do you find yourself backing up, hanging your head, wishing he was gone, and feeling really beat up by his behavior? Readying an apology for something you really didn't do wrong?

OR, do you find yourself completely embarrassed by his behavior and don't feel you have the energy to respond to his outburst at all?

OR???

Yes, there are lots of ways you might react.

Wouldn't it be better to **Catch** yourself by taking the time to consider his behavior; then **Check** your feelings and thoughts about what he is saying; and finally, calmly you choose to **Change** your typical reaction into a controlled response, that shows this lout that you are in-control and quite capable of an intelligent, assertive approach to resolving this situation?

YOU have this choice! You have it every time you are in a difficult situation with a difficult person.

Questions/ideas for contemplation

What kind of attitude DO you want to bring to a difficult situation?

Think of difficult situations you have been in recently and **imagine taking these extra moments to stay in-control.**

Can you see yourself making other choices?

Try practicing *Catch it, Check it, Change it* in a variety of situations this week. They don't have to be difficult situations. Just see if you can get the hang of it. You might be surprised at how much control you suddenly have – control of yourself and the choices you make.

Chapter 7

Knowing Yourself

The first of *The Seven Keys to Understanding and Working with Difficult People* is **Self-Awareness**. The focus of this chapter will be to take this concept a step further, by offering you a means to understand some key aspects of yourself better.

I believe that we all have the right to be the best we can be, and part of that process is **accepting that our life's responsibilities rests firmly on our own shoulders**. Through whatever difficulties arise, we have to make the best choices for who we are and who we want to become.

Yes, we can blame others, circumstances, "The World," and so on; however, we do have choices – choices we make every day that delineate to others the person we really are. How do you really want to be seen? Who is the real YOU that you want to bring to the world on a regular basis? Who is the person you really want to be at work with your colleagues?

Ask yourself

Who am I and how do I fit into the grand scheme of things?

You can approach this from several perspectives:

Who am I? Deep inside? The real me?

Who do I really want to be?

How am I bringing this conception to reality in this world (at home, at work, with friends)?

Can I bring the inner reality/dream of who I truly want to be to fruition?

I believe the best way to get at who you are fundamentally as a human being, the true you, as it were, is to do a little exercise I developed for my book *Guiding Children*.

Who we are fundamentally is based on what we really value. If we consider the qualities and values that we would want our children to have and develop as they grow up, I believe we are touching the basis for what we truly value in ourselves. Try this exercise:

What ten qualities or values would you like to instill in your children as they grow? Make a list.

Try to be specific and to keep the number at or around ten fundamental qualities. Stick with values and qualities, i.e. don't put in things like, "I want Marsha to be a surgeon."

When you have a solid list, start to prioritize. Pick the top five values you would like them to have; then narrow it to three. See if you can get it down to the one most important, fundamental quality you would like your child to have. Then put the list back together in order of priority.

Chances are this list describes what your ideal of YOU is.

Need help getting started?

At the end of this section is my short list of values that I worked on for my children and myself. However, be sure to consider a wide range of ideas, values, qualities, etc. that fit your vision for your children, for yourself.

Find the best words that work for your self-image.

Initially, you may want to start with a much longer list and then over time work to narrow it down to the top ten best descriptive words for what you envision.

After you have developed your list, print it out and carry it with you or post it in a place where you will encounter it frequently. You can also make a small-print version, laminate it, and carry it in your wallet or purse.

Another Perspective

Another means of understanding what you truly value is to ask yourself these questions:

> How would you like to be remembered?
>
> How would you like your relatives, friends, coworkers, even strangers to remember you? In other words, "How did you impact their lives?"
>
> What would you like engraved on your tombstone – the final comment on who you were?

These are very personal considerations and you may find thinking about them a bit difficult; however, when we are willing to make the effort, it does help us **focus on what is most important**. If you feel it could help, you could discuss this approach with a close friend or relative. When we consider these types of questions, it places our whole life in perspective, and it can give us a fundamental ideal or concept to continually strive for.

Here's the clincher

Put these qualities and values to the forefront of your life. Bring them to work with you. Live them at home, in the office, and even interacting with strangers out in the "real" world.

In every interaction you have,

> How are you manifesting the qualities of your ideal you?
>
> How do you bring what you value most to the fore?
>
> How many moments of your existence from this point on can you live fulfilling this personal image?

The more you can be you, the **you** of your deepest values and qualities, the easier your relationships with difficult others will be… and the more joyous and fulfilling your life will be, too.

As promised, here is the short list I developed for my children and myself.

    Caring, Kind and Loving

    Responsible for their own lives and actions

    Respect and Compassion for their fellow man and woman

    Respect for all life and their own spirituality

    Open and Honest

    Self-aware and Self-confident

    A love and joy of life

    Love of learning and creativity

    Being of Service to others

Make the best possible choices for yourself, and then make the effort to bring this YOU into the world at every opportunity.

Part II
Dealing with Difficult Behaviors

This section of the book focuses on the types of behaviors that often cause difficulties in the work place (Chapter 6); Getting at and Dealing with concerns you may have had with someone in the past (Chapter 7); essential Communication Skills for being successful with difficult people (Chapters 8 and 9); and a more in-depth look at problem behaviors and specific recommendations for being successful with these behaviors (Chapters 10 through 27); finally we will introduce some other ideas and skills for making the most of your work life and your interactions with others.

Chapter 8
Outline of Difficult Behaviors

The list of difficult behaviors presented in this chapter is drawn from a wide variety of sources included in the Bibliography and from my own personal experiences as a Coworker, Coach, Counselor, and mentor. I used a list from Leonhard Felder's *Does Someone At Work Treat You Badly? How to Handle Brutal Bosses, Crazy Coworkers...and Anyone Else Who Drives You Nuts*, as a jumping off point.

These behaviors cover a wide gamut of concerns we have with difficult coworkers (and others); however, this certainly is not an exhaustive list. Feel free to add to the list any words or phrases that help you specify more closely the type of behaviors that concern you the most.

As we discuss types of difficult behaviors throughout this book, we will group similar terms together for ease of discussion and approach, e.g. Dishonest, Liar, Insincere, Deceitful, Cheating. Much of what we discuss will relate back to the Key Ideas presented in the first part of this book, *The Seven Keys to Being Successful with Difficult People*, and the **Communications skills** discussed in Chapters 10 and 11. The focus of this section of the book will be on how **to apply** these ideas to specific difficult behaviors.

Aggressive, Passive, and Passive-Aggressive

I discuss difficult behaviors in several of my other books in terms of how they fit into these three categories. These provide another valuable perspective in looking at difficult behavior. It can be useful to look at specific behaviors and see how they relate to these three categories:

Aggressive Behaviors are those that are direct and 'in our face.' There is nothing subtle about aggression. Anger, explosions, tantrums, bullying, etc. are types of Aggressive behaviors.

Passive-Aggressive Behavior is behavior that is not 'in your face', but is aggressive indirectly. Back-stabbing, whining, complaining, resistance, etc. are types of Passive-Aggressive behaviors.

Unlike aggressive or passive-aggressive, **Passive Behavior** tends to frustrate us because little or nothing is happening. It is the lack of response that can produce difficult situations. Non-responsive, indifferent, blasé, bored, etc., would be considered Passive behaviors.

The List

Below are related behaviors that often cause frustration and angst between people. These will be introduced here and then will be discussed at length in later chapters as we introduce tools and skills to deal with different types of behavior.

> Note: Word forms – the categories and choices of word forms below are based on descriptive quality. So, while 'a snitch' is not a 'behavior' per se, it seems to work better than 'snitching.' I have chosen what I feel are the most descriptive word forms to present these behaviors.

I highly recommend that you **go through this list at least once carefully**. Consider what behaviors might be relevant to difficult colleagues you work with. Understanding and acknowledging those behaviors that frustrate you can serve as a start place for being successful with them.

Feel free to write in the margins or take notes on items that you especially notice or feel anxious about. This is another means to beginning the process of understanding yourself better, understanding your perpetrator(s) better, and learning to deal with specific types of behaviors.

Controlling behaviors

We discussed this important issue in Chapter 4. **I would consider ALL difficult behaviors to be controlling in one way or another**, i.e. aggressive, passive-aggressive, passive, all are used to attempt to control another person or situation. Take a few moments as you go through these behaviors see if you can see how each behavior can be 'controlling.'

Frustrating behaviors

Behaviors that get under our skin and are difficult to deal with because they are not always out in the open:

Obstructionist behaviors

Behaviors that 'get in our way' in some form or another.

Condescending, Sarcastic, Difficulty maintaining boundaries

Dishonest, Lying, Being Insincere, Cheating, Deceitful

Backstabbing, Rumor Monger, Sabotaging, Vindictive

Snitch, Tattletale, Gossiper

Sycophant, Obsequious, Overly reliant, Co-dependent/Clingy, Cliquish

Con-artists, Schemers, Wheeler-dealers, Manipulative, Game-playing

Impulsive, Intrusive, Snooping

'No' people

In your face behaviors

Behaviors that either rile us up or get us running for cover. Nothing subtle here.

Aggressive, Verbal abuse, Screamer, Exploder, Volatile, Hostile

Irritable, Hyper, Short-tempered, Quick-tempered, Abrasive

Bullying, Argumentative, Intimidates, Demanding, Defensive

'Not quite with it' behaviors

These can be frustrating behaviors because we can't quite understand what is motivating (or not motivating) the people who manifest them. [I actually don't like this category title from a personal standpoint, but it does describe effectively 'How we tend to feel,' when working with people with these behavioral concerns.]

Spacey, Rambling, Inept

Forgetful, Unreliable, Easily Distracted

Hard to Reach, Hard to Pin Down/Won't Make a Decision, Unavailable

Unresponsive, Taciturn, Tight-lipped

Rigid, Set-in-their-ways

'Does anyone care?' behaviors

Behaviors that seem rooted in an 'I really could care less' attitude.

Apathetic, Cold, Uncaring, Uncompassionate

Heartless, Lacks empathy, Insensitive

Blasé, Indifferent, Bored

Clock-watcher, Non-motivated, Slackers, Shirker, Procrastinator

Depressed/Depressive

Over-committing – Under-delivering, Passively resistant

'It has to be right; I am better than you' behaviors

Behaviors that put the perpetrator 'up,' and the victim. 'down.'

Fault-finders, Critical, Derogatory, Put-down, Invalidates

One-uppers, Perfectionist, Always Right, Over-analyzing, Nitpicker

Self-centered, Egotist, Lacks humility

Narcissistic, Self-absorbed, Aloof, Know-it-all

'Can it get any more negative than this' behaviors

Behaviors that seem to always have as a foundation a negative perspective on life.

Whiners, Complainers, Pessimistic, Blaming, Accusing

Rude, Abrupt, Boorish, Obnoxious

Negative, Doomsayers, Curmudgeons, Moody, Sulking

Stubborn, Hard-headed, Selfish

'The world is out to get me' behaviors

Behaviors that have fear as a major component.

Suspicious, Distrusting, Paranoid/fearful, Phobic

Anxious, Overly emotional

Constantly needs attention

'Out there' behaviors

Behaviors that we likely do not understand, or find it hard to accept.

Bizarre, Odd, Weird

'There are laws against these' behaviors

Legally improper behaviors that should be addressed immediately by the appropriate authority at work.

Sexual Innuendo, Advances, Seductive

Inappropriate Comments or Suggestions, Flirtatious

Harassment

Keep in Mind

Whatever behaviors your difficult person manifests on a regular basis, these are the methods that they use to get what they need, want, and desire. As strange as that may seem at times, what is frustrating you is how they get things done, and/or how they present themselves in their interactions with the rest of the world, for better or for worse.

Our goal is to help you to develop the insight into the behaviors that upset you; and through that insight to help you build the knowledge, skills, and tools to get past the past and be able to deal with these behaviors successfully in the future.

Yes, you do want to be able to be successful with this one 'difficult person,' but by focusing on behaviors you will have the tools to deal with similar difficult people in the future as well.

Questions and Ideas for Contemplation

Taking the time to really understand the behaviors that have been frustrating you is a big first step in being able to deal with them. It helps us to understand ourselves and to understand the other person.

An excellent exercise is to print the pages above listing all the behavior types, and then to go through and select or highlight each item that reflects the difficult behaviors you are concerned with, or even those that you know can frustrate you. Make notes about terms that strike a chord with you. Feel free to add terms that better describe your own concerns with an individual. The better you can delineate the behaviors that bother you, the easier it will be to begin to be successful

Ask yourself these questions as you work with your list:

> How do you feel when you encounter/deal with this behavior?
>
> What do you think about when you are 'in the midst' of dealing with this behavior?
>
> What are your typical reactions?

Writing these responses down can be very beneficial. The more you understand how a specific behavior impacts you, the better you will be able to 'see it coming' and to change your response so that you maintain self-control and your self-worth.

Next, take each frustrating behavior and consider how this behavior serves the individual perpetrating it.

> What is their motivation?
>
> How exactly are they trying to affect you?
>
> What are they after? What is their intent?
>
> What are their needs, wants, and desires, and how to they fulfill these using this specific behavior?

Can you better understand who they are and why they do what they do after considering all of this?

Don't forget: **Every difficult encounter with another person, every difficult situation we are in, has the potential for us to learn.** Keeping this in mind can change the dynamics of how you approach the problem right from the start

Chapter 9
Getting Past the Past

Impossible Co-worker?

It is not unusual for many good employees to have very frustrating experiences at work with one or more colleagues. Is there a way to turn these experiences around, so you don't have to carry that burden with you for the rest of your work life? Is there a way to reconcile this job, these relationships, so you can succeed, even if you run into another difficult personality?

Definitely!

You are in Command

Much of what you have learned and will learn while working through this book has to do with your own self-worth and willingness to take charge of your life. We all have things from our past that we would like to be rid of. Moving on with your life and work is not about forgetting what happened, it is about facing it and learning better ways to deal with the same types of concerns in the future. [And you may as well as face up to it, life tends to send us the same curves time and again until we do learn how to deal with them.]

Taking Command

In this section we will discuss some ideas and present a couple of exercises for helping you deal with past or current difficult relationships at work. These exercises can help you face many of the concerns you have had with a given individual and prepare to face the future with more self-confidence and personal integrity. As you work through these exercises think about how you might apply *The Seven Keys to being Successful with Difficult People*. These are the basic concepts and understandings you need to use to take command of how you feel about the past, so you can feel confident about moving ahead with your life and work.

The Past can HURT!

While I have both a counseling and coaching background, the emphasis here will be toward the coaching side of things. Counselors tend to spend a great deal of time focusing on and analyzing the past. This can be very useful if there are deep-rooted concerns that affect your ability to effectively relate to people. Our focus will be to look at recent concerns you have had with difficult people and the difficult behaviors they manifest; as well as to take a look at your reactions to those negative behaviors, so that you can eventually let those tensions and anxieties go, and move more positively ahead with your work relationships.

Awareness of our feelings, thoughts, reactions and of, as much as we can, another person's perspective can aid a great deal in our working positively and constructively with the ideas and tools found throughout this work.

We want to focus on:

> What, very specifically, was troubling about the relationship you want to get over/through.

And,

> How you dealt with the relationship and behaviors at the time.

When you understand these concepts, you can move ahead with your life. And you can be in a much better position to learn skills and techniques for being successful in other difficult relationships you may face in the future, or to deal with a current relationship more positively.

"This relationship was DIFFICULT because..."

The first step in getting past a bad relationship with a former colleague is to:

Understand the frustrations you had

and to

Specify the behaviors that caused you so much angst

One of the best ways to get at this type of relational information is to **write about it**. Take the high-lighted statement above and write an answer to it, then another, and another. [You can do this on a computer or do it long-hand. Writing everything out longhand sometimes helps us get into the process even more.]

E.g.

This relationship has been (was) DIFFICULT because...

> Steve was always pushing me around.
>
> Steve lied to our boss about things I had accomplished, or would take credit for my work himself.
>
> And so on.

You can also make this more personal from the start:

> My relationship with Steve has been difficult because...

Try different approaches, but keep working at it. Write answers that reflect your frustrations, anger, sadness, and so forth; as well as answers that delineate, in as much detail as you can remember, the behaviors that this person exhibited that frustrated you so much.

Be specific, be detailed, and make yourself do this until nothing else could possibly come into your head. Then come back an hour, day, or week later and add to what you have already done. The more you can get out and write down, the better. You are essentially making a hard-copy of everything that was not right about your relationship with this person. You are also, in a sense, reliving your frustrations, which can be very cathartic and releasing.

Caution: This type of work can be emotionally trying. If you feel this may be too difficult, or if it troubles you a great deal, please seek professional help before proceeding. Professional insight and support can be invaluable in working through this process. Counselors or specially trained coaches can provide the help you need.

More Examples:

> This relationship was DIFFICULT because... this colleague never had anything good to say about me and the work I did.

> This relationship was DIFFICULT because... this guy would explode over nothing and I would somehow always seem to be right there to 'catch it all.'

> My relationship with Steve is DIFFICULT because... he was always talking behind my back, telling lies about me to others and I had no idea how to put a stop to it.

Take the Next Step

For every item you wrote down in the above exercise, every response you made, write down a brief statement (paragraph) about what your typical reaction was to 'X' behavior or 'X' Frustration. Write about your feelings, your thoughts, and your reactions -- both outward (physical) and inner (emotional, psychological) reactions.

Examples:

> This relationship was DIFFICULT because... my colleague never had anything good to say about me and the work I did.

> I always felt really demeaned and worthless in this job. I even found myself fishing for compliments and never got them. I became depressed and had to go on medication. Eventually, my work quality suffered, and I just didn't care anymore.

List everything that you can think of about how this impacted you:

This relationship was DIFFICULT because... this guy would explode over nothing and I would somehow always seem to be right there to 'catch it all.'

> I hated these times. Overall this guy was an okay person, but when he exploded all hell broke loose. I felt humiliated even though most of the time it wasn't my fault. I wanted to run and hide every time I saw him storm out of his cubicle. Sometimes, I felt physically ill. It really got bad toward the end and I missed work because I just didn't want to face him and his negativity.

> My relationship with Steve was DIFFICULT because... he was always talking behind my back telling lies about me to others and I had no idea how to put a stop to it.

> I just got angrier and angrier; and even though I denied everything I heard; I knew people were beginning to question my integrity. I talked to my boss, but he said I needed proof. Sometimes, I just wanted to scream or lash out at this person, but I am too professional to act like that. I ended up just avoiding him whenever possible.

Read what you have written

Take a step back from all of this when you feel you are done. After you have put a few days behind you, go back and read everything you wrote. You will be surprised at how different it feels to look at it from this 'new' perspective. Now that you have it out and down on paper, it becomes so much less volatile. This process can help you can stay in command of your feelings and thoughts when dealing with this person in the future, OR, when dealing with a similar personality later in your work life. Looking at your relationship with this difficult person can help you develop your 'difficult people' skills, so you can deal with this type of personality/these types of concerns better in the future.

VERY Important!

Make sure this information is kept in a secure location, far from any prying eyes. Keep it private and personal. You may share this or parts of this with your coach or a very trusted friend or colleague if you feel that would be helpful. Coaches trained in working through difficult people concerns can offer you considerable insight. It can be valuable to go through specific areas with a coach or another trusted professional, especially those behaviors that really 'pushed your buttons.'

Revisit these notes after you have gone through different parts of this book, and consider what skills and tools, what overall approach will help you deal with these types of difficult behaviors in the future.

Another Exercise

It can also be valuable to write a letter to your 'difficult' person after you have completed the exercises in this chapter. **THIS LETTER IS NOT TO BE MAILED!** It is for your own benefit.

Write down whatever you feel. Sometimes it is cathartic to write two letters:

> One in which you 'let it all out' and rant and rave and say whatever you couldn't say in person. Really try to get at your emotions go, and say what needs to be said.

> Then write a second letter (either right away or in a day or so) and make an effort to forgive this person for how they have treated you. Let them know that you understand that they have their own 'stuff' they are dealing with. Tell them that you are professional enough to take a step back and understand that the past is past. Let them know that you plan to learn from this relationship and move ahead with your life. [NOTE! **Don't mail this letter either**, unless you discuss it first with a trusted colleague, coach, counselor, or friend. Most of the time, it does not serve any purpose to send these types of letters.]

Finally: It can be very releasing to read these letters out loud (to yourself) or with a coach or very close friend – someone you trust implicitly. You may also find it useful to have a short ceremony where you burn the first letter and release this relationship and its difficulties from your life.

The Point Is...

You are opening up and facing the challenges of the past and taking a good, honest look at how all that affected you. When you have done this, it is like you have taken a huge burden off your shoulders and can look much more objectively (and in-control) at those past concerns. You will be freer to learn what you need to learn to help deal with these types of difficult relationships in the future. Read-on. Your new approach to difficult colleagues is next.

Questions and Ideas for Contemplation

Don't forget that all of this self-work is private. Be sure to keep your work private unless you are sharing it with a trusted professional: executive or personal coach, counselor, clergy member, mentor, etc.

The more you face all the concerns, inanities, difficulties, frustrations, etc. you continue to have with a difficult person in your life, the easier it will be to work with all the skills and tools that follow in this book.

Chapter 10
Communications

"Listen without Judgement" (Perkins)

"Respond without Blame" (Koob)

Our ability to maintain our self-control with a solid sense of self-worth is fundamental to being successful with difficult behaviors. We manifest our inner strengths in our outward communications, both verbal and non-verbal. Permeating all of our literature at difficultpeople.org is a solid core of good advice about positive and effective communications. In this chapter and the next, we will reintroduce many of these ideas with a focus on interacting with colleagues in the workplace.

Keep in mind throughout your interactions with everyone, that the choices you make can dramatically affect the choices the other person makes, REGARDLESS of where and with whom the concerns may have started. Only when we buy into a person's negative, disruptive, poor communications and behavior do we lose all chance of making a difference and changing the dynamics with this individual for the better. You CAN be in-control of YOU. 99% of the time that is all that it takes to turn things around.

How we interact with difficult people sets the stage for whether we can be successful with them. Communicating with any difficult person requires skill, finesse, honesty, and kindness.

Communicating with a colleague adds a slightly different dimension than your average difficult situation because typically you spend a fair amount of time and effort with this person in the work place. If you are at odds on a regular basis, it creates many concerns in your own ability to work well and contentedly. It also can create a negative atmosphere that permeates line and matrix teams and can even affect the whole division or organization. Quality and productivity can suffer. People are affected emotionally, psychologically, and even physically.

Your interaction with a difficult person at work can have more purpose than succeeding with what you are working on together. You can:

    Learn a great deal about yourself in the process.

    Learn as much as you can about who they are and what their intent is.

    Continue to develop positive and useful communication skills and techniques

IMPORTANT: Listening is your most important tool.

Listening

Everyone wants to be heard and to be understood. Many difficult relationships start because of poor communications on the part of both 'participants.' I am going to go out on a limb here, but I firmly believe, and I have studied and taught communication skills for a long time, that none of us listens as well as we could/should. I include myself in this mix!

Unfortunately, we all, also, tend to blame the other person for poor listening skills, when we may be at least partially responsible ourselves.

We all can learn to listen better.

We call can learn to communicate better.

It is very easy for us to lose attention, skip ahead, hear something not as it was meant but as we interpret it (because of our own stuff), get bored, etc. I know personally that I find myself thinking miles ahead of what someone is saying. I am very creative, and as someone talks, I am thinking up things at a mile a minute. Sometimes that causes me to lose the heart and soul of what they are trying to get across.

Poor listening and poor communications can come from down-home stubbornness. We just don't want to 'give in' and try to understand something from another person's point of view.

Good listening skills go beyond just hearing words. Good listening skills go beyond hearing the meaning your colleague is trying to get across to you. **Good listening skills get at the heart and soul of what is important to the person you are interacting with, i.e. understanding who they are, their needs, wants, desires, and their intent.**

If you want to avoid difficult situations or temper an already difficult encounter, you have to let them know you are listening, really listening. Below are listening skills that go an important step beyond listening and hearing to 'being with' another person.

Listening skills

A variety of useful tools that help show interest and understanding are always at your disposal.

In Person:

>Lean slightly forward. It shows you are interested and 'there' with them.

>Stand at a comfortable speaking distance. Don't get in their space or their face, even if they are in yours. Take a step back, if necessary, to create a comfortable distance. Stand erect, be self-confident, but don't show aggression; and try to be relaxed, even if the other person isn't. **Mimic a stance and posture that you'd like them to take.**

>Maintain eye contact, but without challenge.

Use nods, your eyes, and movements of your head to denote listening and understanding. Keep hands relaxed and gesticulate to emphasize points without showing aggression.

Use silence as a tool; allow them time to respond to you. Give respectful silence when you feel it is needed to allow them to collect their thoughts. Hint: far too often we feel it is necessary to 'jump in' and fill gaps of silence. Sometimes, it is best to hold back, or say something that encourages them to go ahead: "That is great, Bob. I'd like to know more."

On the Phone and In Person:

Part of listening is feedback; simple 'yeses,' 'uh-huhs,' and 'nods' work well. It also pays to go beyond these important forms of feedback by being more definitive, "I hear what you are telling me," "I understand," etc.

You can be more effective by occasionally repeating back what they are telling you (backtracking). When you repeat an important phrase, idea, bit of information, back to a person it tells them, beyond any doubt, that you have heard what they have said. You can go overboard with this, but most of us don't do it enough. Rephrasing to make sure you understand is a great tool, too.

One of the keys to backtracking is to focus on important information or ideas they are saying and to give them feedback on key points. Backtracking in this way is a form of acknowledgment and can also be perceived as a form of recognition.

Use their name occasionally. This helps acknowledge who they are and helps them to feel you are focused on them.

Colleagues with Concerns

When a coworker approaches (or calls) you and is obviously not a happy camper, you can be assured that their feelings are part of the picture. Listening for and acknowledging a person's feelings can help defuse a disgruntled or even a volatile colleague.

Try to visualize what they are trying to get across to you. "Painting" a picture in your own mind of their concern, situation, and frustration will help you understand far better what is driving their behavior. (Case and Rhoades-Baum)

Feelings

Understanding and acknowledging the other person's feelings are key skills in effective communications. They are particularly helpful when working with a difficult person.

Be willing to "Say it":

> "I understand that you are very upset about this. Can you explain a bit more about...?"

A simple statement like this and the ones that follow can immediately change the dynamics of a discussion. You are establishing that you care about how they feel; that can, and often does, change another person's 'difficult' approach.

> "I see that you feel really bad about this, Alyce. I do want to help if I can"

> "I am very sorry you are angry. Please let me know what I can do to help..."

There are many ways you can phrase your initial communications to someone's concerns to let them know you are **attentive to them** and want to help.

When you do it with compassion and kindness, most people, even difficult people, will respond more positively. Edginess will dissipate, difficult behavior will ease, and your 'difficult' person will then be in a position to communicate more effectively and kindly, too. They will also be in a position (mood, attitude) to listen to you, which very likely wasn't on the agenda a minute before. They may even be willing to listen to solutions you may have to offer to their concerns.

In essence you are showing them that you care – about their concern, about how they are feeling, and about working toward a solution with them. You are letting them know that you care about their needs, wants, desires, and intent.

Taking Communications a Step Further

Listening is the start. Good communications continue with good observation, i.e. **paying attention to yourself and to the other person you are interacting with**. How you present yourself can make a major difference in how effective and successful you are in working with a difficult colleague.

Pay attention to their voice, posture, and gestures. This will tell you a good bit about what they are feeling and how the conversation is going.

Key point

People know when you are involved in a conversation or not. They pay attention to your tone of voice, posture, and gestures. Even if your contact with them is strictly by phone, they can 'see' how much you are involved with them by what you do and say.

> Pay attention to your own communications: what you say and how you say it

Observe your own communications: improving your communication skills starts with really listening to them and continues with your actively paying attention to what you say and the reaction other people have to how you say something.

Important: Often how we think something is coming across is NOT how the other person receives it.

Our <u>intent</u> does not really matter

IF they <u>do not understand</u> what our intent is.

Communication Skills

Be clear and brief. Time is almost always a factor in conversations. A difficult person may see a long-winded response as an attempt to 'one-up' them and their ideas.

Ask questions to clarify and further understand what they want. Taking the focus back to them is smart politics. Especially if you do have something important to say. When they feel understood, they are more likely to listen to your ideas.

Asking questions is a skill and a tool that you can develop and hone. Practicing, and using good question-asking techniques can be very valuable in being successful with a difficult coworker.

Listen carefully to their reactions/responses to what you have said. It will give you clues to how things are going and how you may direct the conversation next.

How to ask questions

Use open-ended questions that begin with 'how, what, when, who, and where." **Avoid using 'why,'** it is accusatory and tends to put people on the defensive.

> "Why didn't you do this the way I wanted in the first place?"
>
> "Why was the...?"
>
> "Why can't I...?"

These all tend to set the other person up to react defensively.

Instead of "Why didn't you...," try something like, "How can we work together to get this in the proper format for the next division meeting."

> You are shouldering some of the responsibility for helping them solve this concern by taking the obvious blame away; and, importantly, it probably won't cost you anything more than a few more minutes conversation. If things keep going well, you might end with, "if you want me to go through this with you before the next meeting, let's set up a time," or even better, "You sound like you have a handle on this. I am looking forward to seeing the next version."

There are always positive ways to ask questions and explore mutually beneficial solutions to concerns.

Try to **avoid the word, 'but.'** It qualifies and diminishes what they are telling you. AND we all use it far more than we think:

> "I understand what you are telling me, but..."
>
> "That is very interesting Alyce, but..."

Both these statements immediately qualify what the person said to you.

If you need to get them to understand something, ask a question.

I understand what you are telling me and I really didn't before. I was wondering if you could you give me your opinion about how it looks this way?"

Major difference! You have avoided 'but' and you have put the ball back in their court. Remember people like to feel they are in-control of a situation. [Take a close look at this: have you given anything up?]

Seek specificity

The more you know, the better. Your interest in seeking clarity and more knowledge will often be appreciated. It helps acknowledge the other person and their views – acknowledgment is one of the key 'intents' of almost everyone. When you have doubts, when you are still not sure what they are trying to get across, ask.

Asking, used properly, shows a desire to understand and to help.

Asking helps keep the ball in their court; they are able to maintain a sense of ownership and control, and you don't give anything up in the process.

It gives them a chance to give more input, 'be the expert' (Toporov), and feel they are contributing. It shows appreciation.

"What do you think we can do?"

"What do you think we can do to resolve this issue?" (Toporov/Koob)

Ask kindly.

Solution driven

Conversations at work, unless they are simply a passing "Hi! How are you?" almost always have a purpose. Conversations with difficult people usually have a strongly driven motivation behind them. You may not know precisely what it is, but be assured the person you are dealing with is after something.

BIG HINT: 99% of the time you can give it to them without giving anything up (except for perhaps a little ego.)

Working within your own self-worth and self-confidence and by using positive, understanding communication skills, you can find out what is driving a difficult coworker. Try to keep this important point in mind and it will be far easier to reach a solution; and more importantly, to establish an equitable, and even harmonious working relationship.

Solutions are not necessarily the most important thing

Interestingly, while a solution focus is an important element, most people will be appreciative of your efforts to understand them and their concerns. When you **pay attention and listen**, a great deal of difficulties will likely to flow away.

Questions and Ideas for Contemplation

Make an effort this week to 'be with' various people at work by paying close attention to what they say, how they say it, and see if you can understand where they are coming from (their intent, needs, etc.) as the conversation progresses. This is not an ostentatious display of outward interest; just try to be genuinely interested in them and their concerns.

Pay attention to yourself during these interactions and see how you are doing and how this changes your own thoughts and feelings. Getting good at this does take practice. Try a few short 'rounds' each day and when you feel more comfortable, see how you feel when interacting with someone you have had concerns with in the past.

If you want, you can keep a diary of notes about how things are going and the progress you feel you are making. Keep it confidential.

Chapter 11
Communicating with Difficult Colleagues

"Circumstances (always) dictate the response." (Weiss)

"What in my heart do I really want to say to this person?"
(Perkins) (my emphasis)

'Difficult' coworkers frequently create angst in others through their approach, their attitude, their negativity, and so on. When you can stay within yourself and **maintain your self-worth, self-confidence, and self-control** in spite of what they do and say, you can be successful with them. Keep in mind that change takes time. It will take you time to learn to remain calm and in-control when someone is trying very hard to push your buttons; and it will take time for the other person to learn that their tactics are no longer going to work with you, i.e. you are not going to let them control your peace of mind through their negativity.

Negativity breeds Negativity

Rude, obnoxious, volatile, depressive, put-down, behind-your-back folks do exist and do impact our world. Have enough negativity enter your day and it will affect you. Keep in mind, too, that any reactions or responses you have that are in anyway negative will add to the mix. This perspective leads to two Key Rules in dealing with difficult coworkers.

Rule #1

Pay Attention to yourself during any interaction with a person you feel is difficult. Pay attention before, during, and after your interaction with them.

To your emotions

How do you feel as you face interacting/working with them?

How are you feeling as you interact with them? What specifically is troubling you?

How do you feel once the encounter is over and you have time to assess the whole experience?

To what is happening physically

Before, during, after – Are you tense? Were you able to remain calm and relaxed? Do you have a headache? Is your heart pounding? And so on.

To what you are thinking

Were you able to focus on work issues, or did this person's behavior/demeanor drag you into their negativity? Could you remain calm and stay interested in what they needed, wanted, cared about; and then were you able to stay in-control and get work completed effectively with them?

To where you are at psychologically

What about them is affecting you and how?

How is their behavior affecting your ability to work?

What do you have to do to maintain your positive, in-control demeanor in spite of who they are and how they are approaching you?

Rule #2

Pay Attention to them.

Everything above in Rule 1 applies here as you relate specifically to the person you are interacting with.

Where are they at emotionally?

Can you get a sense of what they are thinking?

Knowledge is a powerful tool. It can be a very positive tool in dealing with a difficult coworker. As you develop your ability to perceive quickly and efficiently where they are emotionally and what they are bringing to the table, you can learn to use this information to help move the interaction in more positive and productive ways.

Defusing Negativity

Having read all the materials up to this point in this book, you now have the understanding and tools you need to move difficult encounters and difficult situations with fellow coworkers into new space with them. The communication skills in the previous chapter are critical to being successful. There are also additional skills and tools you can learn that can help defuse really negative and even volatile interactions with someone else.

IMPORTANT: Always work from a **safety-first** perspective. If a situation has the potential to be seriously threatening to you or others, seek help. Be sure you can handle the situation if the other person is angry and/or very negative.

Never put yourself or other people at risk.

Let them know you are with them

Repeat their name over and over:

"John... John... I am listening... John, please try to calm down. I am paying attention and I want to understand why you are upset."

There are two key elements to this type of response to negativity and volatility.

You are getting their attention focused on you, which most often will take them out of their 'stuff' and get them to lower the stakes.

Be sure to get their attention, kindly.

You are letting them know you are paying attention to them and are ready to listen and understand.

Let them know in some way that you are paying full attention to their concerns.

When you do this, it also helps take you out of your 'stuff,' and lets you focus on choosing a better response to their 'button pushing' behavior.

Showing this type of interest and respect will catch the attention of almost anyone and bring them into a much different space with you. It shows you are trying to 'be with them.' They probably will also realize you are aware of their negative behavior and are not buying into it. Do this enough times and they will change their tactics with you. They almost have to, because they are no longer getting the reaction they expect and want. Note: some difficult people take longer than others to get the idea that you aren't going to get angry or cower to their outbursts anymore.

Once you have their attention and they have calmed, you can use the communication techniques you have been practicing: self-control, listening, understanding, positivity, etc.

Another calming technique is to move to a different 'battleground' as soon as you can, if it is feasible. You could suggest taking a walk with them, going to a neutral spot where you can talk freely, i.e. not their office/space and not yours. Plus, movement can have a calming effect by itself. When you move to a neutral space, no one is more 'in charge' than someone else.

Make sure you stay calm and in-control, even if your insides aren't. It generally does take some time to train yourself not to react inwardly to the nasty things other people do and say. Eventually, you can get to the point where their negativity just doesn't make a difference to how you feel! Avoid any hint of frustration, negativity, or aggression on your part, no matter what they have been doing or are doing. Keep on top of your outward demeanor, expressions and gestures, as well as what you say. You don't need to be passive or feel like you are giving in. You want to be assertive, in-control, and as positive as possible.

First focus on their concern

If they are upset, pushy, demanding, blaming, etc., you may very well want to react to that negativity. Instead, try to center yourself and then try to understand what they are after. Even if they are putting you down, you can still get them to focus on specifics and get away from the blame:

"Can you help me understand what you feel is wrong?"

"What can I do to help?"

"How can I make this better?"

"I understand you are very upset about this, help me to understand what is wrong and I will make every effort to work through it with you."

"Is there anything I can do to make this work out better for you?"

And so on.

You are trying to give them a chance to unload, without you being the victim of their stuff and their poor communications. You can even...

Apologize

Yes, it may seem like the furthest thing from your mind when someone else is putting you down or screaming at you; however, you can use a fairly neutral statement that goes a long way to mollifying their upset and concerns. Typically, you don't even have to give in, admit to, or give up anything to do this.

> "I am really sorry you are upset. I am sure we can find a way to fix this."

> "I am sorry this isn't the way you want it. Is there anything I can do to get this back on track?"

> "I am sorry. I know you are frustrated. Let's work this out. I'd much rather find a way for us to work together amenably."

Here you have added a caveat that you'd rather deal with their concerns in a different, more professional and amiable way.

> "You are right. I didn't see that problem. It is my mistake and I will fix it. I appreciate you pointing that out to me. You really are a good editor and that helps the team be its best."

If you did do something 'wrong,' which a nitpicker or perfectionist is sure to jump on, you can almost always throw them off their blaming routine by coming back at them with something totally unexpected, i.e. admitting you messed up. [They **expect** you to get upset, fight back, etc.] They may continue to nitpick, but you will probably get more respect and a calmer approach in the future. You are always laying the groundwork for future interactions with a difficult person, not just focusing on solving today's problems. (Duston)

Let them talk

Very often a frustrated, picky, demanding, i.e. difficult person just wants people to pay attention to their concerns and to them. They seek acknowledgment and understanding. If we give them the opportunity to really unload a few times, their difficult behavior may change dramatically and even disappear. Why? Because we've helped fulfill their needs, wants, desires, and intent. All they really wanted was a concerned ear.

Let them wind down by truly listening – being 'with' them. Don't interrupt unless they ask a question and expect an answer, or if they pause and wait for a response. Take the opportunity to reinforce that you have heard what they said (backtracking, repeating key points). Keep in mind that silence can also be a good technique. When you are on top of the conversation, you will quickly learn when to interject something and when just to listen.

Your willingness to let them speak first and freely, shows respect for them, puts them 'in the driver's seat' in a sense, and helps further defuse a volatile situation. It also gives you the opportunity to learn something about them and what is motivating this concern. Most people will respond to this type of approach in a much calmer and more positive way themselves.

When it is your turn -- respond

Reacting means you give up control.

When we react negatively in a difficult situation, we are giving away our self-control, our power, to the other person. We are buying into their negativity and letting it drive us out of our self-confident, positive stance. No one likes to give up control, but we do it all the time when we become defensive or when we let someone else direct/affect our emotions, thoughts, and actions.

Anger, frustration, tension, upset, guilt, defensiveness, and all negativity that comes from our interaction with a difficult person are indications that we have given over our self-control.

Responding means we are staying in-control.

When we can take an instant to stop and check what we are feeling and thinking, and to become aware of the action we are considering (our typical reaction to this type of negativity), we can make other, more positive choices. Then we can maintain our **self-control**.

Bring it all together

When you feel you have given the person the opportunity to speak, and you understand what they have been trying to get across, it is a good practice to get into the habit of briefly summarizing what they said. This can reinforce the notion that you have been paying attention to their concerns by listening carefully to them. It also gives them the opportunity to 'correct' any misconceptions they feel you may have. It keeps the ball in their court a little longer.

At this point, you should be free to let them know what you are thinking and how you feel. Do it kindly and positively:

> "I think I've really got a handle on what is important to you now. Would you be willing to listen to some of my ideas on this? Maybe we can find some way to incorporate what is most important to both of us."

> "Your ideas are great, Eleanor. [It doesn't hurt to give some kudos. Really, it doesn't!] Could I show you something I think is important to add to this?"

Most people, even difficult people, respond well if they have first been heard and feel they have been understood and acknowledged.

Yes, there are a very few people who are so insecure and negative that they can't get past their own stuff and who are unwilling to consider anything except what they want. [We will discuss working with really difficult people near the end of this book.] However, don't assume this is the case until you have given your difficult person the benefit of the doubt several times. You have to be willing to try these positive, self-confident, in-control techniques for several weeks, or even longer with some people, before they will acknowledge through their actions that your relationship has changed. They may have a good bit of 'stuff' from the past to get through before they start to come around.

Important: Anything less than a 100% positive, person-focused approach won't work. Difficult people will often jump on anything, even the smallest thing, that they deem is negative. Remember, that how they look at the world is vastly different from you. They are likely coming from a position of poor self-esteem. It is not your responsibility to fix them or even put up with their negativity; but think about how good it will feel if you can change your relationship for the better, and positively influence their work/life in the bargain, **because** you have maintained your self-worth and positive approach.

Learn from them

You can learn a tremendous amount about the person you are interacting with by being open to listening to their side of the story. You can learn what is important to them: their needs, wants, desires, and intent. You can learn what motivates them and their perceptions of the world, which you are likely to find are much different than you thought. You can also learn why they are upset or generally negative, which will help you make better choices in working with them in the future and on a regular basis.

You may learn, and while this may seem very surprising right now, that you have made a friend.

Thank them

This is the simplest communication tool of them all and it is too often left out. It is very effective. Thank them for their input, their honesty, and their willingness to share. Thank them in some way. It is kind, positive, and it can make a big difference in how your next interaction with them begins.

Finally

Most people who approach you negatively will respond to the techniques delineated in the chapters above. Give them a chance to respond differently to you. It may take some time and more than several positive interactions with them. Keep in mind that all positivity that you add to your work life with them, from this moment on, can help the situation. Sincere forms of acknowledgment, praise, attention, and effort can make a difference in how your work with this individual goes. [See Chapter 30, *Things You Can Do to Make a Difference*.]

Questions and Ideas for Contemplation

Communication skills are the means in which we use the *Seven Keys to Being Successful with Difficult People*. [Self-awareness; Self-worth; Self-confidence; Self-control; Honesty; Kindness; Positivity]. As we work through the types of behaviors that cause considerable problems in relationships at work, we will show how these techniques and skills can be applied to specific concerns.

These are great, basic communication techniques. Please keep in mind, however, that they work only if you can remain in-control, calm, and positive. **It also helps immensely to be kind.** These techniques require a good bit of practice coupled with constant work on self-awareness. Mental practice, i.e. envisioning, imaging scenarios with a difficult person, and/or revisiting troublesome encounters you have had before with this individual, can be very valuable.

Chapter 12

Controlling Behaviors

This chapter is a brief, more in-depth look at the issue of 'Control' in relationships. As mentioned earlier, every difficult behavior we will discuss has an element of control or 'who's in-control' as part of the dynamics.

The only true control is self-control.

Self-control comes from Self-worth and Self-awareness.

Difficult people

People who regularly exhibit difficult behaviors are using them to control and manipulate others. They can demonstrate outwardly aggressive and demanding forms of control, or subtle, behind-your-back, passive means of control. They use these 'techniques' to get what they want.

Really difficult people may be using a particular behavior just to get a reaction from you. Their self-esteem is so poor that the only way they can satisfactorily interact with the rest of humanity is to put other people down. They may even reach a point where they enjoy seeing other people squirm, or fight back, or cower.

Regardless of how difficult and negative their behavior is, the only choice you can make if you want to have a positive, effective working relationship with a peer is to maintain your self-control. If you give in to defensiveness, anger, a fear impulse, or other negative reaction you have handed control over to them.

A colleague cannot control you without your permission.

No one can **make** you feel anything.

We have the power

We always have the power to make positive, assertive, self-affirming choices, or something else. Choose wisely.

Do you need to be right?

Another important concept that is directly related to control issues is **the need to be right**.

When we use positive, people-affirming communications as discussed in the two chapters preceding this one, we are in essence often allowing the difficult person in our life to maintain their illusion of being in-control (while maintaining our self-control) and we are letting them feel they are holding the strings. We are allowing them **to be right**.

Most of the time this costs us nothing. But boy is it hard to see that, unless we are really in-control and on top of ourselves during the interaction.

Most of us have a deep-rooted need to 'be right.' We try our best to preserve it at all costs through our ego. Consider this example:

> A colleague, who has been very negative and verbally abusive to you in the past, charges into your office and starts ranting and raving about what an idiot you are and how you have totally screwed up the 'Baker' contract.
>
> You have put considerable time and effort in the Baker contract and you know that it is fundamentally sound. You had to send it to this difficult colleague for input at your boss's suggestion. Now you are getting a stream of verbal abuse, as you expected, because this colleague has never found anything good to say about your work.

How do you react?

Most of us would get defensive and fight back.

> "Come on, Ben, I put a lot of work into this contract. I really resent..."

This is probably the mildest form of a reaction you might have. Use your imagination or remember how you have responded to this type of behavior in the past. Or, if you are not feeling very self-confident, you might 'flee.' (Bend over backwards to placate Ben; feel bad, etc.)

> "I am really sorry. I tried to do my best. Look, I will work on it tonight again. I am sure I can do better... Sorry... Really sorry, Ben."

Can you think of other ways that you might 'give in' or 'give up' your control to this person?

There are better, more-confident, in-control ways of dealing with this person and you can help him to 'be right' without your really 'being wrong.'

Try something different

Stay in-control and respond:

> "John, John! Please calm down. I am listening. I really want to understand what you are upset about. If there is a concern, we can surely work it out. Come on in and have a seat. I will give you my full attention."

You haven't admitted screwing up. You have handed him the reins by offering to hear him out, i.e. he feels 'in-control,' and you have very likely defused a good bit of the negativity right off the bat. Now you can use those great communications techniques you have been practicing and really get to the bottom of John's wants, needs, desires, and intent. Maybe all he needed was to feel in-control and to have some genuine attention paid to his ideas. Chances are you have begun to change the permanent dynamics between you for the better and your next interaction will be different.

Giving up 'control' or 'pseudo-control' costs us nothing 99% of the time; and if you think about this issue in depth, even the times where our need to 'be right' is critical, the use of positive, in-control communication techniques can get us there.

Two types of really controlling behaviors

Two of the difficult behaviors on our master list have the over-tones of being very controlling: **obstructionist behaviors** and **people who always say "No,'** to everything that isn't their idea.

Both these types of behaviors, which are often coupled with other difficult behaviors, can be extremely frustrating to deal with. How can you get someone who is always trying to block you, or says 'No' to everything you bring up, to change their ways?

Let them win

One way is to let them win. This doesn't mean you give up on your ideas or even change them. There are a number of ways you can help someone else win and still get your way.

Help them become part of the solution

People will bend over backward to get something done if they own part of it. An obstructionist person can be brought on-board by letting them have their say, really hearing them out by listening carefully to their input, and then by helping them to be invested in the solution.

Bring your ideas into the mix through the back door

> "Alice, you have great ideas, I particularly like your take on how to market this widget. What do you think about adding to this by... (insert one of your ideas)? This would enhance what you have suggested and it would probably appeal to the boss even more."

Help them be part of the problem

This is a great technique that comes earlier in the whole process.

> "Lisa, I have a problem I am thinking about in regards to the Eckard proposal. I could really use your input. Would you be willing to hear my ideas and then give me some help? I think the boss would appreciate your input, too."

Once someone is invested in a problem, they are more likely to listen more agreeably to possible solutions. Always give them the opportunity to be heard, to add ideas, and to feel they are acknowledged and recognized (or will be) for their work. Let them be a part of it.

Always let them have some sense of control

When people are vested in a problem or in finding a solution, they are more likely to feel they have some sense of control in the whole process. That, and some form of acknowledgement, appreciation, and/or recognition can make all the difference in the world in how they work with you and others.

Always let them 'be right' in some way.

Don't give up what is important to you. Just be sure that what you want is grounded in your most positive values and qualities and not in your ego. Then it is much easier to find ways for obstructionist people to be right and be in-control. Which in turn can result in your getting things done effectively and efficiently.

These approaches are far better than, "I want to do this," or "This is the only way it can be done," way of doing things, which is often our ego talking.

When all else fails

There are a few individuals in the world who are just plain obstinate. Certainly, try using your best communication techniques in trying to get them aboard what you are attempting. If you have made a concerted effort, i.e. you have given them plenty of opportunity to give you their ideas and input, and you have tried to invest them in your ideas, yet you are still running into a roadblock, then move ahead as kindly and positively as possible.

There are times when the best thing is to move on. Here's a way to do that without burning too many bridges:

> Memo or e-mail: "John, you have been a great help with the Eckard proposal with the ideas you have shared. I am ready to move on this and since I still feel strongly about the (insert your idea/solution), I am going to send it up to Fred and see what he thinks. I will let him know how you have helped with the project and also let him know some of your reservations to my ideas. I really appreciate the time you have spent on this. [Saying 'Thanks' never hurts.]

This approach acknowledges John and his ideas in several ways, which is very important to establishing a good working relationship, while still affording you the opportunity to move ahead and do the quality work you feel you need to do. It helps John get some credit with the higher ups and even though you are disagreeing with him, you have done it respectfully and kindly.

Most people, even difficult people, will appreciate this more positive approach.

Thinking things through

Many of the solutions to difficult behavior concerns we will discuss throughout the remainder of this book will be based around applying the *Seven Keys to Being Successful with Difficult People* and the communications skills discussed in previous chapters. **There are always ways to present and approach things that neutralize negativity and add positivity to the mix.** Always!

Questions and Ideas for Contemplation

Have a 'No' person in your work life? Try visualizing a scenario (past or future) where they try to block an idea of yours. How does the conversation develop? What different ways can you couch things that give your difficult person some ownership and feeling of being in-control? Can you imagine a productive, satisfactory outcome by using positive techniques?

Practice helps!

Chapter 13
Frustrating Behaviors
Key Ideas

We all have dealt with frustrating people in our lives. Some people just have a way of getting under our skin with their negative approach; and since they often do this in a surreptitious, under-handed way, we find them especially hard to deal with.

It is all about ATTITUDE

Well, it really is a lot about attitude. Our **positive self-worth** plays a major role in being successful with these behaviors. One of the keys to working with this type of behavior is to take a step back and do a self-appraisal. Ask yourself this question:

How/why is this person's behavior bothering me?

Then answer the question very specifically.

"I am getting very frustrated because John is always talking to others behind my back. People tell me some of the things he's said, but I don't know what to do, since I don't have any proof. It is his word against theirs and they are not willing to stand up to him if push comes to shove. I get angry and tense. I am losing sleep, and I know I've gotten more irritable here at work and even at home. Sometimes I just want to scream..." And so on.

This guy has gotten under this person's skin. Through his negative, behind-the-back tactics, he is creating a great deal of upset and perturbation. Their self-worth and confidence in being able to handle this person's behavior has taken a major hit.

First things first

With all negative behaviors we need to take a short period of inner strength time and get back to our center – the values and qualities we truly believe in for ourselves (see Chapters 5 and 7). This is especially true for frustrating behaviors because they tend to be some of the hardest to deal with, and can slowly and often very destructively affect our well-being.

In a sense, you need to say to yourself:

"I am not going to let negativity impact my self-worth!

This may seem silly, but it IS very important to think about 'getting your life back,' i.e. 'taking charge of YOU.'

Here is a useful analogy:

When we are sick, especially a prolonged cold or other drawn-out illness, it often drags us out of our normal positive, in-control self. That is because in many ways we feel we don't have **control** of what is going on in our bodies. If we really look at it objectively, we probably realize don't have much immediate control. However, most of us will do everything we can to alleviate our misery and find ways to get past this physical concern. We will take medicine, get extra sleep, seek information, go to a doctor, take vitamins, eat better, etc. If you believe in any type of self-healing, you may do some meditation, exercise, positive thinking, and so on. Generally, we will keep seeking ways to feel better, so we can get back to normal.

One very important element to healing and moving ahead with our lives is our **attitude**. We could give in to our misery and wallow in self-pity, or we can be proactive and make the most of where we are for this moment in our life. Even if our illness is chronic, we have this choice.

Attitude changes everything.

In the same way, attitude – how we feel about ourselves – affects how we deal with difficult, frustrating behaviors.

Fear and low self-esteem

It is most probable that the negative behavior you are putting up with is driven by your difficult person's low self-worth and their fear of 'being found out.' Many difficult people exhibit, or 'use' difficult behaviors to put other people down, and thus, by elevating themselves in their own eyes and perhaps, they feel, in others' eyes as well. They are often not consciously aware of doing this.

When we can keep this concept in mind, it helps us maintain our own center. They are hurting inside, probably a good bit. They haven't developed a way to handle their own concerns and it comes out in the form of negative behavior perpetrated on other people. You happen to be one of their current victims.

I am a person who has always wanted to help other people. When I keep in mind that the person I am dealing with is rooted in their own poor self-image and inner pain, I can approach them and their negative behavior with a completely different attitude – **an attitude rooted in my own self-worth, self-control, and kindness**. This opens the door for me to be able to deal with them successfully and it goes a long way toward taking me out of my frustrations with their behavior.

Remember!

We can't change their behavior directly and we shouldn't expect them to necessarily change who they are in general. Our goal is to change our own actions/attitude, so that they change their behavior toward us. We can handle their negative behavior with aplomb and kindness because we are POSITIVE, IN-CONTROL, and SELF-CONFIDENT.

Sometimes a difficult person will change their negative behavior for the better because they see in us a more positive, in-control way of living and working. I say this very cautiously because it shouldn't be an expectation. If you effect such change, it typically takes a long time and it takes a long-term commitment to positivity on your part. ANY negativity or perceived negativity in your relationship with them and they will most likely revert back to old ways.

Positivity does breed positivity and it CAN have an effect on an office or group of people, but it takes a truly remarkable, consistently positive person who is capable of maintaining their centeredness through all forms of negativity. I have seen it happen. One outwardly shining positive personality can change a work atmosphere quickly; so can one negative personality – that is where the persistence comes in. **Stay positive and other people will notice. Stay positive long enough and a lot of people will notice and want to come on board.**

Eventually the negative person will face some hard choices: come on board; be alone; or leave.

Keep in mind as you read through the rest of this book about dealing with specific difficult behaviors that difficult people tend to resort to other negative behaviors if their preferred behavior isn't working. So, while their in-the-face shouting may cease if you refuse to react to it, they may try being manipulative and vindictive as a means of gaining attention and boosting themselves. However, if you stay on your own positive course, eventually they will have no choice but to take their games and negativity elsewhere, or to change for the better. Most difficult people will take what they perceive is the easiest route, which unfortunately, is often to aim their games in a new direction. That is why setting a goal to 'save' another person or to 'change them for the better' is not very realistic.

Things you can do to stay positive...

while in the face of negativity.

You have stepped back your frustrations and delineated the behaviors that cause them, and you have gotten your feet back on the ground. What is next?

Build a personal support network:

Spouse, significant other, or close friend who you can confide in.

This is very important, especially when dealing with deceptive and deceitful behaviors. It helps to talk things out.

A **trustworthy colleague** can also be a sounding board and offer considerable support, especially if they have been having the same frustrations as you have with this person.

Make sure this is someone you feel you can confide in without any concerns. Keep in mind that offices are very limited spaces and walls do seem to have ears. Keep your discussions/sharing confidential and make sure you both understand this pact.

Be positive in your daily work: there are many ways to effect positive change in everyday tasks: kind words, thanking people, memos, etc. [We will discuss these types of ideas in more depth near the end of this book.]

Write: **document** concerns, feelings, things that happen, etc. Keep it very private. This can help you in making things more concrete and by giving you something you can refer back to as you make progress. Keeping a daily log or diary can be valuable. Writing can be very cathartic. It also can also provide documentation if you ever need it.

Take care of yourself. Treat yourself for staying positive and in-control. Privately celebrate your successes.

Professional support also can be helpful: coaches will help you stay on track, bolster you in difficult times, and offer assistance and ideas to help you make positive choices; counselors can help you deal with deep-rooted concerns and frustrations; clergy and other professionals may be where you need to turn if you feel the need.

Getting help is smart and it can make a big difference in staying the course, especially when dealing with undermining behaviors.

Moving ahead

Next, we will look closely at a wide variety of frustrating behaviors. More specific ideas and skills will be discussed and many examples given of ways you can approach these types of concerns. There is considerable overlap in terminology and in approach. **Techniques we discuss relevant to one behavior may also prove very effective with another.** Keep in mind that you are building a repertoire of tools and skills that you can use in many difficult situations.

Note: throughout the rest of this text we combine similar types of behavior for the ease of discussion. Therefore, it is wise to spend some time specifically detailing the behavior(s) of the difficult person who is troubling you (and others). Then you will know better how to deal with it. Use the many examples in this book as a jumping off place for understanding the behavior you are concerned about, as well as for knowing what tools, skills, and techniques to use to help in overcoming this frustration.

It is worth reiterating one key point from above – frustrating behaviors are particularly hard to deal with because of their deceptive nature. Thus, making the effort to detail your concerns is especially important as a jumping-off point for being successful with this type of difficult behavior.

Dishonest, Lying, Cheating, Deceitful, Insincere

I once worked with a person who could tell a bald-faced lie to your face, you could call him on it, and while still looking you straight in the eye he would shrug his shoulders and change the subject. Most liars or deceitful people are not this obvious; much of their behavior is surreptitious. How do you deal with this type of behavior when it is so hard to pin down?

Get ready

You want to have all your ducks in a row before working on being successful with a dishonest type. Make sure you are grounded in your own positive values, that you have carefully outlined the behaviors that are frustrating you, and that you feel you have built a support network as you prepare to dive in.

Document, Document, Document

It is wise to plan on documenting as much as possible everything you hear in regards to this person's behavior, particularly when it impacts you, everything that is done within your purview, and everything that happens in your interactions with them. This can be hard to do because it does take time and so much of what frustrates you about them is 'hearsay' or 'probably(s).' However, it can help a great deal to make this effort.

> It can give you a running documentation of concerns both you and others have if you ever have to take this to a higher authority, or stand up for yourself in light of some mis-truth that has been spread around.
>
> It gives you concrete materials you can refer back to for your own consideration and efforts.
>
> You will have some very specific reference points if you are ever questioned. "Bob, you told me on January 27th at our meeting from 3:00 to 4:00 p.m. that you had taken care of the Parker account and paid the bill." Direct documentation like this can halt a dishonest person in their tracks. It may not stop their behavior altogether, but they are going to think a bit more about trying to pull the wool over your eyes.

Be honest; be kind

This person has significant problems or they wouldn't be using this type of behavior to make their way in the world. We can always remember to be kind and we can always find more positive ways to broach things.

Consider this:

> Beth comes into your office and in the course of your interaction you ask her whether she sent an important e-mail delineating recent data to fellow matrix team members. She answers, "Oh yes, I sent it out yesterday morning."
>
> You have the following confirmed information:
>
>> You are on the mailing list and didn't get it.
>>
>> Steve and Sven both told you this morning that they were still waiting for it.
>>
>> Beth was out all of yesterday 'sick' (a neighbor told you she saw her at the mall at 1:00 PM); she hadn't taken her computer home; and you know she doesn't have e-mail access in her apartment, nor a personal computer other than her work laptop.

Think this is farfetched? It isn't. Deceivers rarely get their cards called, and it is not unusual for them to just fall into the habit of telling a lie for convenience sake rather than face up to a failure on their part.

> You could: call Beth on all these points, make a 'thing' out of her lies, and in the process make an enemy out of her
>
> OR
>
> You could try something like this: "Beth, I need you to be completely truthful with me as we work together. Otherwise I can't do my job well and neither can the rest of the team. If you don't have time to get something done, let us know and we will find a way to help when it is

this critical. I haven't received the data yet; nor have several other team members who called me this morning. Maybe it got tied up in the system. Whatever the case, let's work on this together right now and get the ball rolling. Please be sure in the future to double-check that everyone received the information on time."

This type of approach lays some things out in the open but **also offers support and help**. You are not blaming her, though she is most likely at fault, not the system. You have given her an 'out'. Beth now knows you are **paying attention** to what she does and she also knows what you expect. It is not likely that her behavior will change because of this one incident, but it is a start. The sick day wasn't brought up because it would have added a great deal of blame and tension to the mix. Plus, as a colleague, unless you are in charge of sick leave, it is not your business to police it. It is something you can document, but leave it at that.

A more **positive, honest, and open approach** can work very well over time. Your goal is to let the person know, as kindly as possible, that you don't tolerate lying, cheating, or any form of dishonesty, and that you are paying attention and will call them on it. If the behavior persists, use this technique again and again.

If it doesn't get any better over time, several weeks or longer, then you might have to have a 'tough love' session with the person. This could be handled like this:

> Set a neutral ground to have a meeting with them.
>
> You can do this on your own, but at this point it might be valuable to get Human Resources or your boss involved.
>
> You want to prepare by getting your documentation in order. Share whatever you feel is appropriate with Human Resources/boss if they are involved.
>
> Make sure the person understands that you are looking for a solution to their behavior and that you are willing to support them in any way necessary for them to make the personal changes necessary for you and your team members to feel comfortable with the working relationship.
>
> Talk openly and honestly about what you expect in the way of a change in behavior. Don't bring up specific incidents unless necessary and then, keep them to a minimum. Just sharing the knowledge that you have documentation in writing can send a very strong message. [Hint: be sure your documentation is always very secure.]

Sometimes showing you care and want to help makes a BIG difference. You could end up with a difficult coworker becoming a supportive colleague because you have approached them **kindly**. Keep in mind that this behavior is a habit and they may slip up or fall back into old ways even though they are trying to change. If you have the confidence of another colleague(s), you can get them on board to help with positive change, too.

Important: Liars and dishonest people are not necessarily outwardly negative in their behavior. They can be very friendly and even loquacious while they tell their fibs. It has become such a habit that they just 'fill-in-the-blanks' when the truth doesn't suit them very well. It is not really a conscious decision, so much as it just flows out as a means of protection.

Con-artists, Schemers, Manipulators, Game Players, Snoops, Cliques

Some people seem to like to play games. They can't keep their hands out of everyone else's business and make it a point to get their way by dealing behind people's backs. They are often at the center of cliques of people who seem to have nothing better to do than complain, worry, blame, and otherwise spread negativity throughout the workplace.

The techniques discussed relevant to dishonest types are applicable here. **It is important to get the behavior(s) that is frustrating you out in the open**, so you can kindly confront them with what they are doing and how it affects you. You have a right to stand up for yourself and to let them know that their games are upsetting to you (and others) and that you would appreciate straight-forward, honest, and open behavior in the future. Make sure you **document** everything you can.

Manipulating types can be very frustrating. They can swing things in their favor by their underhanded methods and you can be left standing out in the cold. Your strongest 'weapon' is your own positivity and values. **Negative cliques and wheeler-dealers don't stand up well in the long run against a really positive, assertive, open, and honest person.** As long as you don't buy into and play their games, or try to play counter-games of your own, your positivity will very likely win out over time.

Use honesty and openness as a tool. If they are being dishonest or wheeling and dealing, open the issue to whole office scrutiny. Talk about it with everyone, keeping things as positive as possible. Call a meeting of interested parties to discuss it – make sure you invite everyone including the schemers and clique members. You want everyone to have a say and to bring it out of the rumor mill. This is an excellent technique for behind-the-back, rumor concerns, too. If it is out in the open, there is not much left to whine and complain about.

It is also a good tactic to call them in for an open discussion.

> "Ellie, I'd like to talk with you about the concerns you have with how the team operates. I think you have some valid points and I think we could spearhead some changes together if we make the effort. Let's talk this out."

> 'Bang.' You have thrown the door wide and brought the issue out in the open. You are offering this person an opportunity to help make changes based on <u>their</u> concerns, and you are being proactive about discussing the problem and seeking solutions. This is so much better than:

> "Ellie, you are really upsetting me and the team with all this underhanded talk about how inefficiently we operate. You especially seem to have problems with me. Why don't you get on board or get off the boat altogether? I don't want to hear any more of this type of stuff going around or I am going to the boss."

Guess what this does? It makes Ellie even more of an enemy, puts her on the defensive, and very likely will send her dealings even further underground. Now you could have a real 'backstabber' on your hands (see below). And guess who will go to the boss first?

Remember: When people can buy into a problem and/or look for a solution to a problem, especially if you are there to help get it going, they are much less likely to be a problem.

You want to nip this type of behavior in the bud – there are ways to do that openly and kindly, ALWAYS.

Backstabbing, Sabotaging, Vindictive Behaviors

Dishonest, under-the-table behavior is at its worst seen in the person who undermines others at work with their negative, vindictive behavior. A person who sabotages you and/or others at work can cause a tremendous amount of turmoil and angst. The ONLY successful way to deal with this type of behavior is **to bring it out into the open**. Let the person know you are aware of their methods. You can still do this as kindly as possible, but **you do have to stick to your guns**:

"Bill, I don't know if this is true or not and I want to give you the benefit of the doubt, but I have been told by several people that you are taking full credit for the Argyle report and that you told others that I didn't do anything on it and even got in your way. Could we sit down and talk about this? I know you will want to tell me your side of this and I'd like to give you a chance to explain, because we did some really good work together on this."

Bill could follow this up in any number of ways: denial (very likely), wants to know "Who told you this," sugar-coat things, get angry, etc. It doesn't matter what tact he takes, remember you are positive, in-control, and you have many good communication techniques at hand. Stand your ground, remain positive, and go with whatever direction this takes. Your aim is to let him know you know what he is doing and that you are not going to tolerate it.

Find a way to end with something like, "Thanks, Bill. I appreciate your willingness to talk with me about this and letting me know your side of the story. Please be sure to come to me directly in the future if you have any concerns with my work or me. I am always willing to get to the bottom of things." That takes the onus and direct blame away but it still lets him know what you want him to know. He'll get the point.

Important: **Never give away your sources of information to a difficult person/colleague.** Document everything, but keep it to yourself. If you need it, you will have it. If this was told to you in complete confidence, you need to protect that confidence. Plus, one person, one incident, doesn't make a truth, no matter how much you trust or feel you should trust your source. Giving Bob the opportunity to tell his side helps ease the blame, and yet, it lets him know you are paying attention and won't let this kind of behavior slide.

Sometimes all they need is...

acknowledgment, attention, and to be heard and to be understood. When we give it to them their secretive, undermining behavior may lessen or even stop. The more positive attention you give them, the less likely they will seek negative attention – believe it or not this is almost always the case.

Really negative behind-the-back behavior

With any of the behaviors we discuss in this section of the book there are always extremes. There are some people who don't seem to care what you or others think, how you feel, and they enjoy upsetting the apple cart. While the solutions we are suggesting may work with them over the long haul, sometimes other things will need to be done in order for a possible positive balance to be reached in your work space. We will discuss extremes of difficult behaviors near the end of the book (Chapter 29).

Sarcastic Behavior, Back-handed Compliments

Don't you just love these types? Nothing like a little sarcasm to start the day. The problem is we are not always sure what they are getting at and how to take it. If we are sensitive at all, it hurts. Hear this kind of thing enough and it gets under your skin.

I had a person in my life who excelled at back-handed compliments. This person could witness something I did and come out with a 'sort-of-compliment.' Here's an example:

(This took place after a performance I led.)

> "That was pretty good, but it wasn't as good as ____ (insert name of famous person).

Well, duh!

What is their intent?

I often wonder with this type of behavior what is the desired result? Does a sarcastic type aim to get the other person riled up? Is it a game they play to see what reaction they might elicit? Or is it just one more example of a person who has **a poor sense of self-worth and needs to put others down in order to raise himself up?**

NOTE: This is a very common reason for difficult people being difficult – low self-esteem. Their defense is to, in essence, attack other people.

I think in many cases sarcastic behavior and the use of backhanded-compliments are subconscious means for a person to raise their own poor self-image up in relationship to the person they are putting down. As with most difficult behaviors it has become more of a way of doing things for this person, a habit, then a conscious effort to put other people down.

There are some people who derive pleasure from seeing other people squirm and they probably do plan ways to 'get at' you or others just for the fun of it, but I truly believe they are in the minority.

Self-worth

Start working with these types of negative behaviors by realizing that the person who uses them on a regular basis probably has very little true self-value. Also, realize that your greatest strength and tool for dealing with sarcasm and behind-the-back compliments is your own self-worth.

Their silly put-downs are not worth the time of day or any investment of energy or emotion on your part. And I do mean silly. If you examine sarcastic statements or back-handed-compliments most of the time they are pretty stupid considering the circumstances. [For instance, why would I want to compare my performance, if I was a little-leaguer, with Mickey Mantle? That is how inane many of these types of comments are.]

When you deal with this type of negativity, get centered in your own values and qualities and try not to let their 'stuff' bother you.

Easier said than done

This isn't always so easy to do, especially if the behavior is pervasive and you get hit with it on a regular basis. There are other approaches you can take, too, but keep in mind the ever-important idea that unless a difficult person's behavior elicits the response they are looking for, it may very well disappear – at least toward you.

You always have two key and very effective tools readily available for working with almost all types of difficult behaviors:

>**Don't react at all.**
>
>**Respond in a way they don't expect**, i.e. positively and in-control.

Things you can do, specifically:

>**Shrug it off**
>
>Smile, nod, and or don't say anything; go back to work. Make sure you keep on top of your own emotions and inner reactions. If this does bother you, then you need to spend some time considering how it has affected you. Don't stuff your feelings.
>
>Just **ignore them** like they didn't say anything and change the subject.
>
>**Look bored.** This can be very effective, though it may trigger their trying again because they can't believe you would react this way. Eventually they will decide it is not worth their effort.
>
>Even better is to: **Stand up for yourself, kindly**
>
>Give them your best genuine smile and say something like. "Alan, I am not sure what you are getting at with that comment, could you explain it to me?
>
>**Asking for an explanation** is warranted, and if done non-confrontationally, i.e. watch your tone of voice and how you say things, it can be very effective. Do this several times and more than likely they

will stop. They don't want to be put on the spot. And this is far from the reaction they were after.

"Alice, I appreciate your feedback, but that sounded a bit off-color. Was there something that bothered you? Do we need to work something out between us?"

You are indicating that you are open for constructive criticism, but you don't really appreciate the way it was delivered. They will get the point after a couple of responses like this.

Keep in mind that people who are sarcastic or offer back-handed compliments want an easy target. When you won't be an easy victim for them, they will probably go elsewhere.

Avoid negativity

It is always tempting to come back in response to sarcasm with sarcasm. Don't! It will only add fuel to the fire, because they will see it as a put down and the battle will be engaged.

Snitches, Tattletales, Gossipers, Rumor-mongers

Don't buy in

And boy, that can be tough. This type of behavior is **attention-seeking**. The perpetrator(s) use these negative techniques to 'get people on their side,' to gain attention, to 'get back' at others or the organization, and so on. The best way to deal with this type of behavior is to maintain your positivity and values and to avoid paying any attention to the negative behavior while finding ways to reinforce and pay attention to positive behaviors.

Pay Attention; Get things out in the open

This type of behavior takes more than one to tango. Usually there is a major ring leader, the main rumor-monger, but there are usually a group of 'followers.' Here are some great ways to put this behavior on the back burner:

Pay extra, **positive attention** to the peripheral members of this gossiping clique; get things more out in the open by visiting people, chatting openly about issues that seem of concern, etc.

If the ringleader is spreading rumors and negativity, **kindly force the issues out into the open** – suggest a forum to talk about specific issues or concerns and make sure everyone has a chance to discuss things freely.

Kind-front the ringleader (as opposed to confronting): "Carl, you seem to feel very strongly about 'X.' Let's form a team committee to address the issue. Why don't you take the leadership role? I will serve as the secretary and maybe we can put something together to take to the boss."

Expect several possible reactions to this:

"Yeah, well, I am too busy. It is not such a big deal, really."

That will let you know that this person's presenting intent is not the issue; their key issue is to gain attention. Do this a few more times and the behavior may change. If you can find ways to pay him a bit more positive attention throughout your work week, the behavior over-all may lessen.

> They buy into your suggestion because they like the idea and the extra attention they get by being a leader. This helps get them out of their gossiping role.

There are certainly other possible reactions. You have the skills and tools, follow through with this. The important thing is that you have **brought things out in the open** and the person(s) involved is **gaining more positive attention, lessening the need for them to continue seeking negative attention.**

A BIG issue

Acknowledgment and attention are two of the biggest issues for difficult people. In Chapter 30, *Things You Can Do that Make a Difference*, we will discuss many ways you can pay more positive attention to colleagues. It doesn't have to take a great deal of your time and it can change the dynamics of an office space and an individual's negative behavior dramatically.

Sycophant, Obsequious, Codependent, Clingy, Impulsive, Intrusive, Difficulty maintaining boundaries

Some people need a lot of support and attention. They can be in your space so much **seeking attention** that it is hard to get any work done. What can you do with overly friendly types? The last thing you want to do is spend more time with them.

Push back gently and kindly

Some people really need a tremendous amount of attention to feel valued. This is a VERY common concern with many types of difficult people. The truth is you don't have the time, nor do you likely have the emotional strength to give them all that they need. However, there are ways to pay them positive attention and yet, get back some of the space you need.

Pay attention to them on your time

We tend to protect ourselves from overly dependent people by avoiding them, finding excuses to get away, etc. By selecting specific times and ways we CAN pay attention to them, we move more into control of the situation while still maintaining some space.

Examples:

> Send them a quick e-mail every morning when you get in. Say something nice and wish them a great day.

> Drop by their cubicle for a quick hello. Being proactive is a great tool in many potential difficult behavior situations, and it keeps you in-control of the space and time.

> Schedule once a month to have lunch with them.

Compliment, acknowledge, recognize them whenever feasible without being obsequious. Don't wait for them to elicit positive feedback, provide it. Even a simple, "Those are the cutest shoes, Mary," can go a long way to raising their spirits.

They will take as much time and attention as you can give and more. Be honest about what you can allow by telling them, rather than by avoiding them. This is particularly important with 'clingy' behaviors.

> "Carla, I wish I had time today with chat with you, but I have to work on this project. It is due on the boss' desk by 4:00.

Carla will still feel put off. Continue with: "I know you probably feel like I am pushing you away (acknowledge their emotions), but there are things I just have to get done. Let's see if we can find some time to get together tomorrow to chat." (Check your calendar, try not to leave this hanging as she will latch onto this and expect it.) "How about a coffee break at 2:00. I have ten minutes then. I will stop by for five minutes in the morning, too if you are available." (Be sure to specifically delineate your availability. This sets up structure and keeps your work time yours.)

You can also get trusted colleagues to help with paying Carla more positive attention. Let them know the reason why this is important to Carla's overall development as a team player.

Create boundaries, kindly

Beth has stopped by to chat and you are in the middle of an important project deadline. Take one or two minutes to be pleasant and supportive and then stand up for your needs, "Beth, I'd love to spend some time with you right now, but I have to get this contract in the mail today. How about if I stop by for a minute after work, say around 4:45?"

> You are giving them an ultimatum while being kind and offering a carrot at the same time – win, win.

Intent, needs, wants, desires

This discussion highlights the importance of **understanding the intent behind a given behavior** as much as possible. **When we can fulfill the need, the behavior will no longer be useful to the person.** It makes sense and it can work if you stick with a positive approach. It can even be a key to being successful with really difficult behaviors.

Questions and Ideas for Contemplation

Take some time now to write down everything you can think of that exasperates you about this difficult person's behavior and how it affects you. Store this away and come back to it occasionally as you continue to develop your positive self-worth and your skills in working with difficult behaviors. You will probably find that much will change over time... for the better.

Does your difficult person exhibit any of these behaviors? Can you envision an interaction with them in which you take a more assertive, positive tact using the techniques outlined in the past few chapters? How can you use your communication skills in a positive way to build a different relationship with this person?

Remember: Give them a chance to be heard. Sometimes it is really what they want, i.e. their 'intent' is to have someone acknowledge them and pay attention to their concerns). Try paying more positive attention to them in the coming days and weeks and see if the behavior disappears!

This Chapter and many more to follow highlight the importance of *The Seven Keys to Being Successful with Difficult People*. Review these (Chapter 7) and think about some of the specific behaviors mentioned in the last three chapters. Can you imagine how these *Seven Keys* can help in understanding and working with people who exhibit these behaviors on a regular basis?

As you go through the rest of this book, consider the difficult behaviors we discuss in light of these Key Ideas:

Self-awareness

Self-worth

Self-Confidence

Self-Control

Honesty

Kindness

Positivity

Chapter 14

In Your Face Behaviors

See the person as more than his/her anger. (Perkins)

We've all had to deal with short-tempered, hyper, aggressive people in our lives. How do we typically react?

Take a moment or two to think back on how you have reacted to aggressive types in your life before:

> Did you get riled up and 'fight' back?
>
> Did you stand in shock, not knowing what to do, and then sometime after get upset or feel bad, ashamed, angry, etc?
>
> Did you get defensive?
>
> Did you want to run and hide?
>
> Did you feel guilty?

Since I started working at this whole idea of difficultpeople.org and reading and writing extensively on the subject of difficult people, it has been very interesting to observe how I feel, what I think, and how I react. Most importantly, I now rarely actually react outwardly. My first inclination is to step back in my mind and contemplate what I am feeling and thinking, as well as how I want to react. Yes, some types of difficult people can still push my buttons at times, but initially I am able to maintain control and find myself in a position to respond, rather than lose control and react. [See Chapter 6, *Being in Control* on **Catch it, Check it, Change it**]

Using this process IS the first Key to being successful with **In Your Face Behaviors** – **maintaining** enough **self-control** to view the situation and your feelings, thoughts, and potential reactions almost instantaneously BEFORE reacting.

This does take practice; however, when we can stop ourselves from reacting to negative, aggressive behaviors we are accomplishing several things:

> We maintain self-control for a brief period of time. [And hence, we don't give over control to the difficult person we are dealing with.]
>
> We set up the opportunity to make more positive responses. We actually can "choose wisely."
>
> The perpetrator is not going to get the reaction he/she expects (fight or flight)
>
> The dynamics of the situation have changed dramatically from what 'used to be'.

It is their stuff

Boy, is it ever! Their aggression shows their lack of control, their lack of kindness and compassion, their lack of self-worth.

You can do better, because you can maintain **your control, your compassion, and respond in an assertive, kind way**.

Don't take it personally

This is another one of those 'easier said than done' things. In-your-face behaviors are hard not to take personally. Try to keep in mind that typically **their behavior has very little to do with you**, it has to do with their lack of control and their lack of couth. [Note: I had to use this word at least once in my writings!)]

Even if you are at fault, they should know how to control themselves and act in an appropriate manner to a colleague.

Stand up for yourself

There is nothing in the difficultpeople.org literature that suggests you have to give in, give up, or otherwise denigrate yourself to appease others who act like they are better than you. You have a right (really an obligation to yourself) to be you, to stand up for the values and qualities that are important to you. Start with **self-worth**!

Assertive behavior means **being able to be self-confident and in-control** in spite of what anyone else is doing. **There are always kind ways to do that.** Review the communications skills in Chapters 10 and 11) for specific ideas, i.e. stand erect and at a comfortable distance from the aggressor, maintain eye contact without challenge, speak in a normal, firm voice, etc.

Express yourself kindly

We will talk about some specific ways to communicate with aggressive people in the next chapter, but always keep in mind that there are kind ways to stand up for yourself without accepting negativity from others.

Impact

Aggressive interactions can have a lasting impact. Though we may weather them effectively through our personal control and positive communication techniques, they can still affect us. **Pay atte**ntion to how you are feeling and how your thoughts are running after an aggressive encounter. **Take care of yourself.** Mentally and emotionally try to deal with whatever is coming up. Talk it out with someone if it continues to bother you – significant other, trusted friend, coach, counselor, etc.

Irritable, Hyper Behaviors

Some people are irritating because they are 'different,' as well as more aggressive than everyone else. When they exhibit this type of behavior frequently at work, we might see their behavior as irritating, pushy, being a little 'too much,' or just off the wall enough to be frustrating. Dealing with people with these concerns takes a good bit of **introspection**.

Know thyself

It is very important to delineate as clearly as possible what irritates you about their behavior. Differences in how two people approach the world can cause a great amount of angst between them. A hyper person might think you are 'laid back,' boring, not working hard enough, etc., and hence think you are the difficult one. Understanding the way another person interacts with the world and giving them some space to do it in their own way, as long as it doesn't consistently get in your face, is a good perspective to start from.

The simple exercise of thinking this all through – their behaviors and how you react to them – can help change the dynamics and lessen the frustrations you (and they) may feel when around each other.

Avoidance

I don't recommend avoiding people often as a strategy, but initially it is not a bad idea when working with irritating or hyper people. It can give you the space and time you need to work through the whole relationship in your mind and to try to see them and their actions in a new light. While it would be nice if they would do this too, don't expect it. The onus is almost always on you if you want a difficult situation to change for the better.

However, sometimes we can't avoid a fellow worker.

Watch, observe, learn

We can learn a good bit from people who are different from us. I find it intriguing to take a step back and consider what is driving another person's personality – this probably comes from my counseling background. Often, if **I pay attention**, I can start to piece together **their needs and intent** from careful observation, especially when I interact with them and when I see them interacting with others. This type of effort can give you a much better picture of their truth and your own truth, which often can help you deal personally with these irritations without doing much else.

A good bit of understanding through observation can lead to a broader appreciation of them, i.e. you can often can put their actions into a different framework and become more:

> Understanding -- especially understanding differences that cause irritations
>
> See the humor in your differences
>
> Feel sadness for what drives their negativity
>
> Be compassionate about their concerns and problems

And you can learn much more about yourself by being compassionate about their concerns.

Approach

Sometimes everything discussed above just isn't enough to alleviate the tension we feel when working with this type of person. Our next choice is to **approach them kindly and compassionately with our concerns**:

> "Susan, you are such a value to this team. I need to let you know, though, that I get upset when you are pushing so hard and when you get so uptight about even little things. Would it be possible to sit down and talk about how we affect each other? I'd like to be able to interact with you without feeling so nervous and anxious?"

It is a good idea to start out with a compliment and then follow that with your concern and a suggested solution. All of this is fairly non-threatening and aims at being productive.

> "Glen, that is right on the money. I think you have good insight into this issue, I feel like you are ticked off, though. Could we talk about this in a more relaxed setting? Let's go down to the cafeteria and get a cup of coffee and iron the rest of this out calmly."

You are owning your own feelings, expressing your needs, and suggesting a neutral place to finish the discussion.

After a few times of getting them out of their negativity into a calmer, more neutral zone, they may very well become more aware of their interactions with you (and possibly others) and begin to change their overall approach, i.e. they are starting to pay attention to themselves because you have helped them become more self-aware. Sometimes all it takes are some gentle reminders that kindly show them how they are affecting you.

Aggression can be hard to take. Aggressive types are terrific at getting us into a defensive mode.

Take a moment and imagine a hostile, aggressive person in a car who swerves around you in spite of the fact that you are going five miles over the speed limit; then he gives you the finger and shouts obscenities as he passes you. If you are like me, you can get upset, uptight, even angry, and yet, if you quickly take a step back and observe yourself, you can notice all of this instantaneously, let yourself feel your emotions, think it through, and (the hard part) try to let it go. It is their stuff. Life isn't fair, as far as we mortals can tell, and it is far better for us to talk ourselves back into our calm and relaxed existence than to let these types bother us more than momentarily. **Why carry all that angst and negativity around all day (or longer).**

Note: I high-lighted the last sentence because this is a REALLY good point to consider. Is it really worth a good bit of angst to let this lout (idiot..., etc.) affect your equanimity (for hours, our day), when you could just let it go? And! Yes, you can! It is often just about ego.

Let it go! Let go of that angst as if you blew it all into a balloon and let it fly away from you... Imagine it flying away, high above and bursting where it will have no effect on anyone. Then go on with your day with a smile on your face. You will be glad you did; and so will everyone else you come in contact with.

Soon you will reach a point where you can sometimes shrug these irritations off. **Their stuff, not yours!**

Screamer, Exploder, Volatile, Short-tempered Behaviors

Volatile people are often above us in the chain, i.e. our boss, someone with seniority, or those colleagues who think they have authority over others. This discussion will focus on the latter, though the techniques are very much the same even if the person does have some kind of authoritarian edge over us. In working with an authority figure the main difference in approach is to keep in mind the caveat that they do have power over us. [See my book, *Succeeding with Difficult Bosses*, Revised Second Edition available at Amazon.com]

Someone who storms out of their office/cubicle and begins to tear into you for whatever reason is having a great deal of problems with self-control. The good news is, though they can be very intimidating, they are some of the easier difficult people to be successful with.

Some important things to keep in mind

> Their ire and dramatics are **their problem, not yours**.
>
> **Maintain**ing **control** is paramount to being successful with them.
>
> You have to let them know that **you are aware of their behavior** and that it **is unacceptable**.
>
> It is critical to **stay positive** in spite of their negativity.
>
> You want to **be assertive** without challenging them.

Important: volatile types will get even more volatile when challenged.

Put these ideas to the test

Henry storms out of his office and you just happen to be walking by. He lashes out at you and your initial reaction is complete shock, though you have witnessed and put up with this behavior before. He is screaming something. It takes a half minute to figure out it is about the Edgard contract, but you really can't tell anything else.

> Often exploding behaviors catch us by surprise. [Sometimes a wide variety of difficult behaviors can catch us by surprise, especially when we least expect something to happen, e.g. when we are having a calm, productive day.]

We may have an initial shocked reaction. We may recoil, we may even flush and feel our own anger begin to take over. This is natural and probably, unless you have considerable training and practice, inevitable. Don't worry, as long as you don't follow through with that initial gut reaction, you can still save the day and make inroads to being successful with this type.

Catch yourself as soon as possible and go through your routine of seeing where you are emotionally, mentally, and reaction-wise. Then prepare to weather the storm:

> Stand straight without showing any form of cowering or cringing back
>
> Be as relaxed as you can under the circumstances
>
> Make eye contact, if possible, but without challenge
>
> Move to a comfortable, normal speaking distance
>
> Speak in a clear, firm voice. You may have to raise your voice slightly, but keep it as calm and soothing as possible while making sure you are heard, then...

Repeat your colleague's name several times until you gain their attention:

> "Henry, Henry, Henry... Please calm down... Henry? I am listening. I am trying to understand what you are upset about... Henry?"

Most people will start to wind down by this time, if Henry doesn't, keep at it.

> Important: if there is ANY threat of physical harm from this person, back off and get help. Never put yourself or anyone else in jeopardy.

When he does start to calm down, add something akin to the following:

> "Henry, I am with you here. I want to understand why you are so upset; but your shouting is upsetting me, and I can't follow what you are saying. Why don't we go into your office?"

The cafeteria or another neutral zone would be ideal, but you need to get a feel from his current stance whether it would be better to listen right now, or take the time to go elsewhere. He just came out of his office and since it is his 'power' space, he can psychologically, from his standpoint, maintain an edge. That is okay with you. **You are in-control.**

Let him talk himself out. You will probably get an earful, but what you are doing is showing him he can be heard without being ridiculous in his behavior. After you have applied your great listening and communication skills, fit something like this into the conversation near the end:

> "Henry, wow! I can see why you were upset; they weren't being very equitable with you. Please remember, I am always here to listen and help in whatever way I can; however, I would appreciate it if we could approach things a bit more calmly from the start next time."

Here's an interesting tidbit: Many exploders, screamers, and short-tempered people are embarrassed, ashamed, and very apologetic afterward. That is fine, but what you really want to do is not have to put up with the explosion and negativity in the first place.

What you have started

Henry is now aware of your feelings. He knows that you will pay attention to what he has to say. He also knows that his behavior is not acceptable to you. Most of the time Henry, and others like him, will make an effort to change their behavior around you (and often around others). It will very likely take a few more 'sessions,' but surprisingly this type often comes around quite quickly.

A word of caution

Really negative aggressive types may change their outward behavior as a result of your in-control approach, and take their tactics underground. You may eventually have to deal with underhanded or even backstabbing behavior from the same person.

Hostile, Bullying, Argumentative, Abrasive, Intimidating, Demanding Behaviors

Some people use a form of aggressive behavior that is very negative, but not necessarily explosive in nature. They try to control and dominate others by intimidation and bullying tactics. These types can be VERY frustrating and hard to deal with because they are very negative.

Don't put up with it! Don't accept it!

The scenario with Henry above is not far from how you deal with abrasive, argumentative types. However, keep in mind several important points:

> This behavior is much more difficult to effectively change, especially in any permanent way.
>
> They may continue to try to argue, be negative, etc. in spite of your positivity (keep at it, positivity almost always wins in the long haul).
>
> **You have to let them know you will not tolerate their negative approach toward you.** You may have to go to the point of refusing to meet with them unless they are willing to come in with a more positive approach.
>
> Stick to your main weapons: **self-worth, self-control, kindness, positivity**.

Many times, their behavior will go underground when it has been thwarted 'above ground'. Stay alert and deal with this too if you need to (see Chapters 13 on *Frustrating Behaviors*).

A brief example:

> Angela comes in and starts 'in' again. She is complaining about you and others, obviously is itching for a good fight, and is pushing you hard to buy into her stuff.
>
> Smile, be positive, try to get her out of the space she's in. "Hi, Angela, I was hoping to see you today. I am glad you stopped by. [Taking a second's pause here and redirecting the conversation can be a useful technique.] I really love that sweater You are wearing. Where did you get it?"

This is probably the total opposite response she's expecting. You are moving far away from whatever she's griping/pushing about and offering her several compliments to boot. The question, if she takes the bait, also helps move her out of her negative stuff for a moment, into neutral ground.

Don't let her get refocused into negativity just yet:

"Hey, do you have time for a quick cup of coffee? Let's grab something from the cafeteria and take a short walk. There are some things I wanted your opinion on and I know you have the insight to help. We can also talk about whatever's on your mind."

More **movement to neutrality** and the positive suggestion and compliment that she can help you. Key Point: Negativity, especially extreme negativity, is attention-getting. **Your compliments are affording her attention, acknowledgment, and recognition.**

Most of the time these types of tactics will move them from their negative space for this interaction and you may actually have a good, open discussion with Angela as a result. It may even have a slight impact on your future relationship with her, but don't expect the world. Really negative, bullying people are deeply rooted in their world outlook. You should plan on having to use these tactics again and again.

There is hope

In order to have a chance at changing Angela's consistently negative behavior with you, you have to give her what she needs and **fulfill her intent. She craves contact, attention, and recognition.** She also believes she can get things done, have things her way, if she is 'in charge' or 'in-control.' By paying more positive attention to Angela throughout the work week, soliciting her input and feedback, praising her when she helps out, etc., you can begin to move her out of her negative space, at least with you. You can also 'let her win,' while not really giving anything up at all.

Difficult bullying personalities need to feel above others. When we can work intelligently and positively with them, while allowing them to perceive that they are in-control, we help fulfill their need. Our gift to ourselves is our self-worth and our self-control. [See previous discussion about *Being Right* and about *Control*.]

Verbal abuse

All the types of difficult people discussed in this chapter tend to verbally abuse others. It is often a part of difficult behavior, especially aggressive and passive aggressive difficult behaviors. As a counselor and mentor, I have witnessed the serious concerns that arise in people who have been consistently verbally abused during their lives. It is a very serious issue.

It is sometimes quite difficult for people who have been verbally abused to develop a strong positive self-worth. It is nothing to be ashamed of, because if you feel you have struggled with this, it is extremely common in our society. If you are continuing to put up with verbal abuse at work, you know how difficult it can be to remain positive and self-confident in the presence of very negative behavior. There is hope, but it does take a good bit of **patience, time, and self-work**.

The key to developing a strong positive sense of self is **self-awareness**: observe how you feel in any given situation, observe the thoughts that go through your mind, and then think them through. **You have to admit your weaknesses and talk yourself up at every turn.** It is important to know what you need to work on and to **encourage yourself and praise yourself for your strengths**. And, I warrant, if you take a close look at yourself, you have many.

Here is one very important strength that you have: **you have already survived all of this crap from others**. You have! And as you develop your self-confidence and positivity you will be able to not only survive, but cope, win, and eventually succeed, too. Stay the course. I know; been there, done that.

Defensive

Being defensive in the face of any type of negativity is our most common reaction.

Negative/difficult people tend to be very defensive. And here's the kicker: they are most defensive about the very tactics they use to try to get what they want, need, and desire. So, if you are dealing with a defensive person, i.e. a person who gets riled at any hint of negativity, you have to pay very close attention to what you say and how you say it.

Sometimes you just have to say it:

> "Carla, I don't want to upset you, but we do need to talk about some of the problems with the Bosco deal. I know and the boss knows, because I told her, that you have done some great work on this. I am not trying to blame you for anything, I just want to get this right so we can move on this. Please always feel free to let me know how you feel and what is important to you."

> "Fred, I want to get your input on our disagreements on the Harley contract. Could we sit down and discuss this calmly. I am ready to listen to everything you feel is important. I know You are a good listener, so I hope you will hear me out, too."

Give them some space, open things up and be honest about what you want to do, help them feel they have some control, but also leave the door open for your own input. Adding a few carefully selected **compliments** is always helpful and gets things off on the right foot.

Treat defensiveness with kid gloves, but don't try to hide things. The more open and honest and kind you can be, the better things will go. **Building trust** over a period of time **through positive communications** can help alleviate concerns you may have with a defensive coworker.

Unfortunately, many difficult people are VERY defensive. It is how they protect their low self-image. Yet, **they rarely see how defensive they are**. They can be very difficult to work with. Keep working with kindness and positivity. These are your best choices. Even if they don't ever move completely out from their negativity and defensiveness, at least you can make their day and work life easier by your positivity.

Questions and Ideas for Contemplation

I can think of dozens of potential difficult situations with aggressive personality types. Keep the following in mind:

You can choose negativity…

Or you can choose positivity.

It is always your choice. One will only get you negativity in return. The other? If you keep at it, you will find your work life much more enjoyable.

Chapter 15
"Not quite with it' Behaviors
Key Ideas

People who just don't seem to quite have everything together or who reject every effort we make to get them involved at work can be very frustrating to those of us who are efficient and dedicated workers. I actually don't like this category title from a personal standpoint, but it does describe effectively 'How we tend to feel,' when working with people with these behavioral concerns. They can drive "Get It Done" and "Get it Right" people to tearing their hair out (see Chapter 4 *The Difficult Coworker*, section on *Intent*).

Is there a way to get through to these types? To get them directed if they are working closely with you and you need them to be productive and effective? To get some kind of response to them?

There is hope

Generally, there are few really completely unresponsive or incompetent people in the world. Typically, people are hired into a position because they are considered capable of handling a job and they have a personality, or so it seemed in the hiring process, that was conducive to this work setting.

It is certainly possible that something happened in the course of their job that led to their becoming more withdrawn or less competent. It is also possible that they were able to put on a good face during the hiring process and fooled everyone. But in either case, there is still hope.

Patience

If I were to add another key idea *to The Seven Keys for Being Successful with Difficult People*, it would probably be 'Patience.' Being able to stay within yourself and consider the problems that affect another human being, start with kindness and self-control. It also often takes a great deal of patience to maintain those attributes in the face of really difficult behaviors, particularly behaviors that can be very frustrating and take a long time to be successful with.

These seemingly 'Not quite with it' behaviors are hard to overcome. Or deal with, because the person who is exhibiting them finds them to be very effective for what they need – often **a form of protection**. For example, an incompetent or inept colleague may simply have shut down because of a deep-rooted fear of doing something wrong; or because they have never received proper guidance and instruction in their job and they are afraid of looking bad. If they have an 'exploding' or 'volatile' boss, it might be more obvious why this is the case; but it is often very hard to pinpoint the exact cause of behavior because our whole life affects where we are as a person.

As a coach, I have rarely seen a person who couldn't become productive on a team and I have actually never worked with someone as a mentor who couldn't be brought out of their shell. Patience and kindness are key!

You can make a difference

Your positive influence can have a motivating and even energizing impact on these types of concerns. However, keep in mind that this can be a very long and drawn out process. Here are some key ideas:

> **Negativity in any form can drive them back to their hiding place.** Even perceived negativity can be devastating to progress you have made with them.
>
> You can only do so much. Sometimes your organization or boss needs to get involved. Training and guidance may be warranted. A coach can help immensely if they are trained to work with employees with these types of concerns. There are many resources at work. You can help be a catalyst by encouraging a coworker to use them and by supporting their venture as they move ahead. Be careful not to overstep your bounds. Discussions with your boss, Human Resources, etc., should almost always be with the knowledge and permission of the person you are trying to help.
>
> **Kindness and Positivity** go a long, long way in drawing unresponsive, 'set-in-their-ways' people out into the office mainstream. Keep in mind that you have to have an incredible amount of patience; fear is often at the root of their behavior.
>
> You are probably not going to make much progress unless you are willing to **make the effort to get to know this person, spend time drawing them out**, and be willing to deal with many frustrations along the way. There is a world of difference between who you are at this moment in time and who they are. You are trying to help bridge that gap. You have to decide whether the effort and time it will take is worth it.
>
>> Hint: this is great mentor training and can teach you a great deal about some of the things you may deal with if you move up in your organization and have to work with these types of behavioral concerns as an authority figure.

I believe everyone, at their core, wants to be effective, efficient, and good at what they do. Sometimes we humans get lost on our way to our own personal fulfillment. The joy of being a coach and mentor is helping people get back on track. In a sense, becoming a mentor is the job you often tackle in being successful with behavioral problems.

People who don't seem to quite have things together are not necessarily exhibiting bad or negative behavior. However, their behavior can be very frustrating. You can take the viewpoint that this is how they deal with the world at work at this time and it is frustrating to you because you see the world from a much different perspective. That opens many more doors for things to improve than if you blame them for how they are.

Spacey, Easily Distracted, Forgetful, Rambling Behaviors

I am at heart a creative-type and when I am bored my favorite way of dealing with it has been to drift off into my imagination. I run with ideas, scenarios, books, etc. – people probably could label me 'spacey,' 'easily distracted,' and or occasionally 'forgetful.' [Maybe because I wasn't paying attention to what they wanted me to pay attention to.]

Gain their full attention

When something is critical to you and your work, you have to step up and help get your colleague on board. You need to do it kindly, and you need to have patience, because they will often miss your mark of what you want and expect. Give them some time to grow.

Praise never hurts and can help get them more motivated.

> Don't be afraid to say it, "Greg, you are an important part of this project. Can we focus exclusively on this for the next hour? I need your full attention."

Important: adult ADD and ADHD are real illnesses and can affect a person's ability to remain focused and to finish things. **Please don't label anyone unless you are a qualified psychologist/psychiatrist; deal with the behavior.** They could be extremely talented colleagues and given the chance will make every effort to succeed. The key is to treat them as a colleague and human being first and foremost, while taking into consideration these specific concerns. Below are additional suggestions that are very effective in working with an easily distracted person.

> **Break things into small pieces**, both time-wise and content-wise. If Greg can't focus for an hour. Have three twenty-minute sessions.
>
> **Help them to succeed.** There is nothing like success to help someone step up to the plate the next time. Success with this type of personality may mean baby steps for you, but it may seem like a major leap for them. Help them get there and remember to acknowledge and recognize them for their progress and accomplishments.
>
> **Provide lots of intermediate encouragement and support.** It helps them continue to succeed and it is a means for you to check on how they are doing. Careful planning within a fairly rigid **structure** can help immensely in giving them the guidance to succeed.
>
> Expect mistakes, 'spaciness,' and other habitual responses from this person. Focus on the current task and not the long haul. Yes, you would like them to change overall, but that may not be in the cards if you are dealing with a person with a physical, mental, or emotional concern that is not curable. Yes, you may be effective in helping them make considerable progress overall, but don't put that very heavy burden on your shoulders or theirs. Be content if it happens over a long period of time.

All of this takes time. You are committing part of your energy and effort to a fellow colleague not just because you are frustrated with them, but because you care. It can be worthwhile from many perspectives. The great thing about succeeding with a person with this type of concern is that you can feel proud for helping them and for not joining the criticism mill. There is nothing like being a part of something positive when it comes to your work with others.

Inept Behaviors

> Lacking, deficient, inadequate, ineffective, incapable, unqualified, wanting, incompetent

These terms all describe behaviors that can cause considerable angst. How much can we actually do if we are stuck working with someone who just can't handle the job they are in?

I chose the word inept because I feel it has a slightly different connotation than many of these others. From a coach's standpoint, I have rarely, if ever, seen anyone who was completely inadequate at their job; perhaps unqualified or untrained, but not incompetent -- and there is the rub.

> It could be the job.

> It is often an attitude about the job/life in general, more than it is about competence.

> It could be a physical, mental, psychological condition that has happened over time.

> And so on.

It is easy to assign blame for a behavior we see and it is simple to complain and rant about how bad someone is. The real truth is that most of the time we have no idea what is the cause of their behavior, and short of having them get a complete physical and psychological work up, and possibly years of therapy, we probably will never know.

What can we do?

The most frequent cause of **ineptness** at work **is motivationally based**. These folks are just not happy campers. Take away their unease, feelings of failure, their fear of failing, their boredom, etc., and many times you will begin to see a transformation. No, this is not your responsibility, but if this is someone you work closely with, and they may have a marked impact on how you enjoy your workspace and work-life (not to mention your advancement), then it is wise to try to make some positive changes for you and them. Here are some ideas to get the ball rolling:

> Review the recommendations above – both the Key Ideas and the ideas associated with "Spacey, Easily, Distracted, Forgetful, and Rambling." Inept people rarely manifest a single frustrating behavior.

> **Talk to them; get to know them**. It is amazing how even this bit of **attention** can change a person's dynamics in the workplace. You may find out they feel left out of the office mix, or feel rejected by others.

You may find out that they are indeed somewhat over their head, but are willing to try as long as they aren't ridiculed for their mistakes and are given a chance to improve.

Encourage and support them in their efforts to talk with your boss, Human Resources, or someone who might be able to make a difference with their job. Unhappiness is a key component of many less than competent workers. It also could be a 'boss issue,' concerns they have with another coworker, etc. Don't ever force yourself on them or others. Let them take the lead and make changes at their own pace.

Offer your support, **acknowledge them**, and find sincere ways to **recognize them** for their achievements. We all like to win and when we do, it generally makes the next part of our life more enjoyable and easier.

If they feel inadequate at some task, offer to give them pointers, check their work, find a training book for them, and so on.

Whatever you do, don't get exasperated with them. That will drive them further into themselves and destroy any good work you have done. It really does take a major effort to **be positive** and **to pay attention to what you say, how you say it, and how they take it**. If they seem put off or upset by something you have done or said, backtrack immediately and try to find out what and how you can make amends.

When you get involved and take an interest, they will probably begin to make some changes for the better.

It is possible that you could run into a major roadblock, too, e.g. you could face a person who lacks all motivation to do anything but ride their time out with as limited effort as possible. However, from my experience that would be very unusual; people like to feel good about themselves, to contribute, and to have others appreciate them.

Unreliable Behavior

While this is a completely different behavior than the others discussed so far in this section, many of the ideas for dealing with this are the same, but they may work in slightly different ways.

Paying attention to an unreliable type not only **acknowledges them**, but it shows them you care about whether they get things done on time and in the right way. In other words, 'You are not going to let things slide.' That can be a wake-up call, too.

Be willing to let them know kindly their work is important to you and that you can't just ignore their not being up to snuff.

> "Iona, I need your input on the Webster contract by Wednesday afternoon. Make sure you have it to me before you leave work. I know you will do a great job."

Positive expectations, rather than some form of ongoing blame, have a much better chance of success.

Here's a poor example:

> "Iona, I am tired of you not getting your work done on time. I got stuck last week working until midnight because you failed to get me the data in time. Get on this and get it to me by Wednesday before you leave work, or else."

> Or else what? Are you going to rant and rave? Or tell the boss?

> If Iona fails to live up to the Wednesday deadline, your best choice is :

> To talk to her about it. **Be open, be honest, be kind.** Try to get some understanding of why she has problems with reliability issues. It doesn't hurt to ask; and again, you are paying attention in a positive way, instead of an accusatory way.

> Set up some parameters for the next deadline. Try to get her to agree to intermediate checks, to see if she is on task; offer to help and support her along the way; offer to oversee her work so she feels like this will be a success, and so on.

Structure can be a very useful tool in dealing with certain types of 'inadequate' difficult behaviors. The clearer parameters are, the less wiggle-room there is, and the easier it is for them, and for you, to agree that 'X' has or hasn't happened. Then you both can look at what can be done in the future.

It is sometimes hard to be positive and kind in the light of repeated reliability concerns. Still, in order to effect positive change, you need to stick to your guns, and at all costs, avoid blame and complaining.

Remember to make sure you stay on top of how you are feeling – treat yourself for being the positive, kind person you are.

Hard to Pin Down/Won't Make a Decision, Unavailable

Difficult people books often characterize these types as 'Unresponsives.' These behaviors can be very frustrating. You want to move ahead, get things done, and make a difference; they don't want to do anything, or won't.

This is one category I have been very successful with. In a counseling or coaching setting where I ran into a 'tight-lipped, stubborn, resisting person,' I managed to eventually get through and get them to open up. I think it really boiled down to some Key Ideas:

> **Trust** – Establishing trust is very important. Part of this may be personality, willingness to share part of yourself, etc. However, the following also help build trust.

> **Patience** – People will often open up, but it rarely happens all at once, though sometimes it does. Give them time to build trust.

> **Seek positive ways to draw them out.** There is an art to finding just the right thing to say. **Asking questions** that suggest **interest, desire to understand and support**, and that include **compassion**ate reaching, out can work well.

> **Kindness** – this is very important in building trust.
>
> **Honesty** – giving lip service to being honest is not good enough. You have to show that you are willing to be open and honest and you need to be willing to trust the person you are dealing with. Honesty works both ways.
>
> **Openness** – a willingness to be open and vulnerable. This also helps establish trust. Mistrust is a common cause of difficulties between colleagues! And it can underlie many difficult behaviors.
>
> Being **pervasively positive**. When the dialogue does start – always, always choose positivity.

Stubbornness, Rigid/ Set-in-their-ways

Run into a brick wall at work? Some people won't even try to see another point of view. Often, very often, this is because **they feel they haven't been heard, that no one cares about their views, and they feel like no one understands**. Your most important skill is '**Listening**.' [See *Communications* Chapters 10 and 11, and Chapter 12 "Controlling Behaviors," particularly the last section on **Obstructionist Behaviors** for lots of good ideas.]

Most people, when they feel people are really interested in them and what they have to say, will ultimately listen to others. But first things first – you need to build that relationship and trust with them before they will give you a chance.

There are almost always ways to reach compromises or get people involved in important projects and ideas IF you make a positive effort to get them involved -- get them on board the bandwagon and to get them in the right seats. Use the techniques discussed above and in the previous chapter.

Unresponsive, Taciturn, Tight-lipped

It is the extremely rare individual who won't eventually respond to **attention, kindness, and positivity**. You don't have to be best friends (though you may make a friend). The most important point I would like to make here is that **if you don't make the effort, they certainly won't**. Here are some other pointers:

> **Make yourself available.** If you can't give them the time of day, don't expect them to change. **Set up and encourage interactions with them.** Neutral ground and a pleasant venue may be a good starting point. Food (breakfast/lunch/coffee break) can help break the ice.
>
> **Give them plenty of space, room, and time to respond.**
>
> Don't fill in conversation gaps; **wait for a response**.
>
> **Ask open-ended questions/leading questions** -- 'Yes' and 'No' questions may simply get a head nod one way or the other.
>
> Try to phrase things in a **win/win** way, i.e. no negativity; and your comments, ideas, questions all have some form of **positivity added**, e.g. **kindness, praise, acknowledgment.**

Offer to help them – with ideas, work, support, making decisions, etc. But don't do their work for them.

When all else fails, **let them know that you value their input**, but you need to make a decision by "X' time and then delineate your thoughts and ideas. Give them a final time to offer input. [Hint: It doesn't hurt to **document** this process.]

Be gentle, too. You may be dealing with a long history of feelings of inadequacy, rebelliousness, poor motivation, fear, etc.

Care

Your initial motivation in dealing with these types of behaviors may very well come from a great deal of frustration because this colleague isn't doing what they are supposed to be doing and because they are impeding your own work and progress. If you have the courage, and yes, it does take **courage**, and the **heart** to care about who they are, the concerns they have, their feelings, their need to be successful and be a part of the team; then you have taken one of those big steps upward on the scale of being human (at least from my perspective). It is the single biggest factor that will ensure whether you have a chance to succeed.

Question and Ideas for Contemplation

Kindness, acknowledgment, recognition, appreciation, and openness and honesty go a long, long way in the workplace and especially when poor behavior is often at its roots a **motivational concern** in the person exhibiting it. When you can provide some of these elements, **your change of behavior will impact their behavior**. It is not as direct as say, making communication and interactional changes during an interface with a volatile, or picky person, but it can make a big difference over time.

Here's a good hint: if you have a trusted colleague who is willing to help, get them on board the positivity and kindness bandwagon. The old saying 'the more, the merrier' does apply in this case.

A key to working with unresponsive, 'not-quite-quite-with-it' behaviors is for us to **do some real soul-searching about why this behavior is so upsetting to us**. It often has a good bit to do with **how our intent differs from their intent** or what we construe as their attitude. By examining ourselves, we can see what we are bringing to the table as we begin making changes in how we interact with them. This can make us much more understanding and hence, effective.

Self-examination -- a good habit to get into.

Chapter 16
'Does anyone care?' Behaviors
Key Ideas

Most of the behaviors discussed in the previous chapter and in this chapter could fit in the passive or passive-aggressive categories. Because they are behaviors that are manifested more in the background, they tend to be more difficult to deal with, especially initially, than more obvious problems.

I personally feel that passive and passive-aggressive are more (or less) the same thing, they are just different in degree. A passive-aggressive person might be more likely to purposely use a behavior surreptitiously to get what they want, while a passive person may be 'passively resisting,' i.e. it is completely subconscious. In either case, the approaches to being successful with them are very similar.

Passively resistant Behaviors

Stay **positive**; this is critical

Be **patient**

Be kindly **honest**

Be available, don't expect them to come to you, you have to **reach out**.

Add structure – especially for those who have trouble getting things done, are afraid to fail, and need some 'wins' in their column to begin to be motivated.

Offer help and support

Be Patient: More than anything, pay them some attention, as much as you can allow. If that isn't enough (and many times it won't be), get help from trusted colleagues and let the person know you will offer as much time as you can. It pays to be open and honest about these kinds of things, rather than just avoiding someone.

Get them involved – there is nothing like purpose to get someone rolling.

Structure is important:

Strategize with them to plan their road to success

Break things into smaller pieces, shorter blocks of time

Motivation and attitude are key – find ways to help them get back on track and be successful

Acknowledge and **Recognize** them for what they accomplish. Be sincere. You can always find positive things to praise.

Indifferent, Apathetic, Bored, Clock-watcher, Non-motivated Behaviors

It can be very frustrating to have someone on a team who just doesn't seem to care. They come to work, sit around and sort-of do something, though their productivity is at such a point that no one actually gives them anything constructive to do. They have become a major drag on the team's productivity and energy.

Fire them?

Sure, you could probably gain enough support to go to the boss and ask that they be fired, transferred (then you are dumping the problem on another team), or cubbyhole them, but all of this is band-aid work and you are not solving your problems, i.e. the loss of this person's productivity (keep in mind that it is not likely their slot will be filled). Then there are always the legal issues, which most bosses and companies don't want to face.

The truth is Indifferent, Apathetic, Bored, Clock-watcher, Non-motivated people are not 'into' whatever is happening. Yes, there may be psychological or mental concerns, or even a physical concern; but from my standpoint as a coach, it is far better to try to get them out of their stuff and back on the bus being productive, than give up or give in without making an effort.

Indifference is often the mark of fear and/or boredom. This colleague may be afraid to try to accomplish whatever task they have been assigned; or they may not like what they have been assigned, and they are completely put-off by what they are expected to do. There can be many reasons for this: new assignment, new boss, promotion beyond their education and training, promotion beyond their abilities, etc.

You could hope that your boss or Human Resources would step in or do something, but don't count on it. There ARE things you can do.

> Most importantly: **talk to them**.
>
> **Pay** them some **attention** and find out over time what is motivating them, or as is more likely, de-motivating them. People like to talk about themselves; and with kind probing, skillful listening, and genuine interest you can draw most people out. This could be ninety-percent of the battle toward getting them back into the main stream of your team's effort:
>
> Find out **how they feel**.
>
> **What is important** to them?
>
> What are their **frustrations**?
>
> Far too often no one ever asks. When I coach, this is the first thing I get into, i.e. **what they need and want**.

Use those great communication skills you are developing. **Listen** carefully and draw them out. Some people are more reticent than others, but I've never met a person I couldn't get to talking.

What isn't happening that they would like to have happen?

Hint: Some reserved people find it impossible to talk to an authority figure, but will open up to a colleague **given the opportunity, attention, and a sense of safety and trust. Earn their trust by being open and honest yourself.**

> What would they like to be doing?
>
> What do they 'get into'?
>
> How do they see themselves as successful and happy in this job?
>
> How could they see themselves becoming more involved with the team?

Some reticent types feel 'left out.' **Helping them feel useful, wanted, cared for, and a part of the team can be the key to success with them.**

It really can be amazing

I have worked with clients who went from feeling ignored, unwanted, discouraged, and far out of the mainstream to turning their whole work life around (and it impacted their life in the real world, too). They not only became involved, but became leaders and started moving up the chain. All I did, in a nutshell, was pay them sincere attention and offer some insights into the world of work and people – much like this book, but specific to their concerns and dreams.

In truth, I believe that many of these types of difficult behaviors develop or are exacerbated because people don't care, or don't seem to care, because they are so busy. Being busy is by far the most common cause of concerns between bosses and employees, because managers just can't seem to break away and actually spend some time with and pay attention to the people they manage but are not really leading. [See my book, *Honoring Work and Life: 99 Words for Leaders to Live By*]

Shirker, Slackers, Procrastinator, Over-committing – Under-delivering Behaviors

These behaviors follow closely the ones discussed in the last chapter with one important caveat – often it seems like they are purposely avoiding work. They can be very frustrating to deal with because we want to get something done and we can't ever be sure they will stand up to the plate and actually do it.

Shirkers and Slackers

There seem to be some genuinely lazy people in life. I have met and worked with a few. Shirkers and slackers and lazy folks do exist. They lack personal motivation and/or just haven't gotten involved with what is going on at work. They just don't seem to care. It may even seem like they make avoiding work a game.

These are definitely behaviors that a boss should pay attention to and make an effort to deal with, but as a colleague you may not want to wait for that to happen. Here are some key ideas that may help make a difference.

Find out what is really going on. **Ask kindly**, but be willing to ask directly. Start the conversation with something positive, a compliment and some small talk, then say what you need to say,

> "Kelly, I want to talk with you about something that is bothering me. I want to see if we can find a solution. You keep missing deadlines we set in the team meetings. You need to understand that this affects the whole team's ability to keep up productivity. Is there anything I can do to help? Could we talk about what your concerns are and how to make this happen for all of us? I really think you could be a top-notch addition to this team if you want to be."

Bring it out in the open. It is your best tactic.

Offer **support** and **encouragement**; DON'T do their work for them. Make sure they understand that what they don't do will be noticed as well as what they do accomplish.

Set **structure**:

> **Set shorter time periods** for reporting what they have accomplished. Whatever seems appropriate and keeps them producing regularly.
>
> **Small bytes** of work that can be done in short periods of time.
>
> **Check all work at every interval. Keep them on their toes.**
>
> Let them know that as their productivity and reliability grow, so will their responsibility and **reward**, i.e. your **appreciation** and **attention**.

Keep letting them know how important their contribution is to the team. Getting them involved, paying attention, providing encouragement, acknowledgment, and showing appreciation and recognition are always important.

Get them involved in what is going on: **the problems and the solutions**. (See also Chapters 1 and 4). When they are invested in the problem and the outcomes, the slacking behavior may completely disappear. **Motivation is key!**

This may all seem like a lot of work for a fellow employee, and something that a superior should be handling/paying attention to, not you. It is, but if that isn't happening, and their work affects yours, then helping your colleague develop may be the single most important thing you can do for yourself at this moment in your work life. Plus, it is educational and rewarding if you look at it that way.

Procrastinator, Over-committing – Under-delivering

Promises, promises, promises.

The procrastinator keeps saying something will be done, but keeps putting it off.

The over-committing person is eager to help, too eager, and takes on much more than he/she can handle.

Either type needs considerable structure and they **need to understand, kindly, how they are impacting the team with their behavior**.

> Help them establish a **work structure that allows them to begin to get things done and to have successes**. This will encourage more structure and effort. Winning small makes all the difference in the world to eventually being able to win big.
>
> Help the over-committing person to **set limits** and **how to say 'No.'** Keep your fellow team members appraised of how much this person can handle and encourage them to stop giving him things to do until he can get his act together and establish an effective and efficient workload.
>
> This type of behavior can benefit from **kindly bringing it out of the closet and into the open**. Get the person to talk about it: their own concerns, feelings, thoughts; and eventually the concerns that you and others have. Reserve a discussion of any depth about how you and others feel about their work until a solid communication relationship has been established with them; then work small concerns that may have persisted into your positive work with them.

Heartless, Cold, Uncaring, Insensitive Behaviors

Some people seem to go beyond not caring about work, they don't seem to care about anything or anyone. It is almost as if they truly do lack a heart. While the rest of the team jokes around, shares personal trivia, socializes to an extent, and generally gets along, this person seems to stand aloof, totally outside the group.

I truly believe that **most people want to be cared for**. I think it is a fundamental human need. Where and how some people seem to have fallen off that boat is difficult to say. Can you make a difference? Probably.

I have never met a person I couldn't find something positive in. Maybe I've been lucky, but I have met some REALLY negative people, too. I have also never met a person I couldn't 'get to' in some positive way. It does take **patience**, lots of **positivity** and **kindness**, and at least enough **confidence** to take some rejection.

These behaviors do require immense patience. Often, we feel that seemingly insensitive, uncompassionate people are aloof, look down at us, place themselves above us, and otherwise keep their distance because we are not 'good enough' for them. The real truth is they are probably very frightened, perhaps unconsciously deep inside, of us and others. **Their demeanor is a protective mechanism.**

The Keys

Lots of positive effort to **communicate** with them

Tremendous **patience** in the face of rebuffs and non-reaction, disinterest

Kindness at every opportunity without being obsequious or bothersome (kind words, kind acts, reaching out)

No hint of negativity

Openness and honesty on your part – it takes this to even begin to get them to open up. It can take a while for them to trust you.

You being you. In dealing with any difficult person, always go back to your own fundamental values, beliefs, and qualities. Then they can see the 'real' you and that is the quickest way to establish trust.

Support and encouragement when they do start to open up.

Depressed/Depressive Behaviors

Depression can be simply a bit of moodiness and sulking; it can also be a serious medical condition. Talking with a down or depressed colleague and regularly **paying them some caring attention** can work wonders – also **showing appreciation, acknowledgment, and recognition**. Be alert to signs of serious depression – down all the time, consistently depressive, self-deprecatory statements, mention of suicide, work quality and attention that has slipped dramatically, etc.

Don't diagnose! Serious mental, psychological, and physical concerns should be left to the trained professional. If you have an established relationship, suggest that they get professional help; you can offer to assist in the process. You can always help a colleague through **caring** and offers of **support**, but don't expect to be a cure-all. Give what attention and support you can, but don't try to counsel a seriously depressed person. **You can be a mentor and a friend. And that can help immensely!**

Questions and Ideas for Contemplation

Don't give up too easily on colleagues who show little interest or motivation. I sincerely believe there is always hope.

If there are more serious mental, psychological, or physical concerns, you can suggest that they seek help, but make sure you do this only after you have established a trusting relationship and when you can sincerely let them know that you are concerned about their well-being. Otherwise, you can report your concerns to your boss, Human Resources, or another appropriate department at work.

Spend a little time every day if you are working with an emotionally draining person by treating yourself to some moments of peace. You can also get support from friends and relatives. Your success with a difficult person may well hinge on how you feel – that always translates in various ways to others.

Chapter 17
'I am better than you' Behaviors
Key Ideas

The problem with this behavior is it really hits us where it hurts. From my personal experience there are few who have such a positive sense of self-worth that these kinds of behaviors don't bother us. The very competitive nature of our society tends to place one person, team, group above another, leaving unfortunately, 'the losers,' to fend for themselves.

At our core, we all have the potential for greatness – greatness for who we are, what we believe, and the goodness of our belief in humanity. When we are consistently told we are 'NOT GOOD ENOUGH,' especially over the course of many years, it has a marked impact on our getting back to that core and our being able to live up to that potential.

Success with difficult people who use 'Put-down' behaviors is founded in these key areas:

> **Becoming more self-aware**
>
> **Recognizing the value and quality you hold deep inside**
>
> **Building your self-worth;** and thus, **building your self-confidence**
>
> Bringing all of these to the foreground in your life

This is the best advice I can give you on dealing with 'put down,' critical, perfectionist behaviors.

Those differences

I have amused myself for years contemplating the 'nature of humanity.' I often have considered at some length the **dichotomy of organizing types versus more disorganized types**. In a nutshell, at the extremes of this 'vision' are the **perfectionist, ultra-organized, have-it-all-together folks** and at the other end **the free-spirited, creative, not-so-organized, 'messy' types**. Most of us fit somewhere in the midst of this continuum, either toward the have-it-all-together side or toward the 'dis-organized side.

Never the twain shall meet!

Many, many differences and difficulties at work and in life are caused because two or more people don't see eye-to-eye. This 'dichotomy' shows one way in which people can get irritated with each other. Free-spirited, messy people, even the moderately messy people like me, don't like to be told what to do, how to do it, and especially that we didn't do it right. Perfectionists just can't seem to tolerate anything that isn't perfect to them. They want everything organized as they see fit and they want it done 'just so.'

I imagine it won't take you very long to think up some circumstances at work where this has been the case for you. Which side of the coin do you hale from? More importantly,

How well do you tolerate the other side?

A perfectionist might scream, "How can you make so many mistakes? Can't you see this stuff and fix it before you send it over to me?"

A free-spirited person might say, "We need to build in some flexibility. If we do it by the book, it will be staid and uninteresting. Get a life!"

Both might throw in a few expletives and snarls if they have been at this type of thing for a while.

Being successful with your opposite requires some tolerance, understanding, and the willingness to accept that it is very, very hard for one type to understand the other. Believe me, it is next to impossible, unless you use some **kindness, compassion**, and possibly a bit of **humor** thrown in the mix.

Another Key point

We tend to see perfectionists, put-downers, always right people as egotists. One question to ask yourself when dealing with these types of behaviors is, "Is the behavior manifested because of the person's attitude/ego or because they are after something, i.e. to get things right? Ego is placing yourself above another person. It is using negativity to deal with others. 'Wanting things to be right' is not necessarily egotistical; picky maybe, but not centered in ego. **It pays to observe the difference.** You may be getting angry at someone because they really care about the quality of things, which certainly can get irritating if its over-the-top; however, true 'put-down' behavior is behavior that aims at making us feel bad or look bad so it raises the perpetrator up.

Dealing with these behaviors

The paragraphs above delineates the foundation for being successful in working with these difficult behaviors. It does take time to **build your self-worth, self-confidence, and self-control.** Keep at it and you will make progress. Practice self-awareness and talk yourself through and past difficult situations and encounters with the types of people who push your hot buttons. Analyze how things went and how your reacted and felt afterward. This is how you will develop strength and confidence over time.

In addition, consider these important ideas:

> Try to understand **what is motivating the behavior**
>> A true sense of concern for quality
>>
>> Or
>>
>> A poor self-image/fear of not being 'good enough' to others.

Another important truth about this type of difficult person is that the very criticisms, negative behaviors they use would REALLY set them off if someone else used them on them.

Stay within yourself as much as possible in spite of their negative behavior. Remind yourself of **your core values**.

This can be very difficult, but it helps a lot. Give in to your emotions later if you need to, don't stuff them. Go ahead and rant and rage a bit at a tree if it helps; or talk things down with a trusted friend.

Talk with them

It is far too often the case that people can't open up about their frustrations with each other. When we can **talk things out openly, honestly, and kindly** a whole ton of negative stuff can wash away. It may be hard to feel like you can initiate this and then actually DO it. However, if you broach the subject, you might be surprised at how open they may be to the idea and it is possible they may be more than willing to mend fences.

Set parameters ahead of time: i.e. we share without judgment, no one interrupts the other, etc.

Talk it all out: how you both feel; share your thoughts; how you or they take something; how you would like to be able to interact; etc. Use **positive communication skills** and be sure to **listen carefully** to what is important to them.

Always be willing to share how you feel in a kind way: "Mark, I am always willing to listen to you, but I often feel, and I know this is my stuff, like you are putting me down when you communicate with me. Maybe you feel awkward with me, too. Could we talk about this?"

Be understanding – they are different from you and quality is one of their key values. Do your best to provide what they want, and go ahead and **let them know you will try your best**. By talking with them you might just be able to reach a position where you understand each other's differences enough to establish an equitable working relationship.

Talk yourself up

It is easy to say to yourself, "don't let their 'stuff'/behavior bother you." It is not so easy to avoid feeling hurt anyway. When you feel you have been put down, criticized, and/or invalidated take some time immediately afterward to work through the whole scenario mentally and emotionally. Then talk yourself up – even if you did make some mistakes look at your positive qualities, pat yourself on the back for all the good things you have accomplished, etc. **Positivity breeds positivity.** We need to work on seeing all the good, effective, and efficient things we do at work and remind ourselves how valuable we truly are.

Fault-finders, Nitpicker, Perfectionist, Over-analyzing Behaviors

Some people seem to revel in finding fault with others. When it is directed at us, or when we see someone else being put-down, it can trigger a whole bunch of sensitive buttons. Here are some other great ideas added to those above:

Thank them

You must be kidding? They just tore me apart.

Actually, I am not. It is the one thing they least expect. Avoid being sarcastic:

> "Neil, I really appreciate what you have said. I will consider all your points. I have been working on this, but I obviously can do better. Thanks, you are great."

When said with sincerity, Neil will likely drop his jaw and walk away, dumbfounded. As strange as it may seem, their tone of voice and how they approach you the next time may very well have changed. They are seeing you in a different light.

Don't cower, get angry, get defensive, or fight back. That is what they may expect if their purpose is ego-based, and it may be exactly what they want – to get a rise out of you. Instead, be assertive, use your best communication skills, and be pleasant. When you don't give them what they want, **listen carefully**, and give your own **calm, controlled response**, they will wonder a great deal about the change in you. After a few times like this, they will change their behavior, at least as far as trying to get a rise out of you. They may even move on to greener pastures, because you are no longer giving them what they need – food for their ego.

Ask them for additional help

This is a great tool that people rarely use. One of the last things this type of difficult person expects is for you to accept what they say and to ask for more of the same:

> "Oscar, I really think you have hit the nail on the head. Would you be willing to check over all my memos and projects? I can see you have a keen eye and brain."

Most likely Oscar will backpedal very quickly. If on the rare chance he takes you up on the idea, so much the better, because now you are directing things in a sense; and if he actually has some helpful ideas, you will look better for the improved quality in your work.

Do your best when under the scrutiny of a perfectionist; **double check your work**. However, DON'T obsess about not 'being perfect' in their eyes. Believe me, it is highly unlikely you will ever get there.

Take these ideas a step further:

> Become a team, you are the creative side, he/she is the quality side; you might make a great tandem.

> Help them become your team's quality control specialist. Then they can pick all they want.

> Offer to have them spearhead all the nit-picky work. They will either back way off or relish the opportunity.

Sometimes the best solution to a concern is to find a creative and inspired answer.

Sometimes the answer to a difficult person is to get them into the right seat on the bus, doing what they love to do anyway!

Addendum

An interesting sidelight to this is that while I have read numerous books about "Dealing with Difficult People," I have not come across any that mention being extremely 'messy' or 'disorganized' as a difficult behavior, and yet I know that messy and disorganized people drive perfectionist types to distraction, often. Just for the record, and in trying to equitable, your best tactics in dealing with a 'messy' or 'disorganized type' are listed below:

> **Patience** – believe it or not most (maybe all) of these types aren't 'messy' or 'disorganized' on purpose.
>
>> I am a good example. While I am not extremely messy, I never quite get my act together: my desk is a mess – even if I clean it; it is back to 'normal' in a day. I leave things around – probably because my mind is always elsewhere. I can read a manuscript ten times and still miss mistakes, that is why I use readers; etc. And I do try!
>
> **Nagging/nit-picking never helps** – feel free to mention something once, but don't harp on it.
>
> **Help them.** Your very best tactic is to tactfully check the work of someone if it really bothers you when they give it to you. Or ASK them if they would like you to check through their materials. If you are nice about it, they will probably appreciate the extra care in making sure everything is right. You can make this even more convincing and amenable by having an agreement to check each other's work. They might develop the habit of checking things more carefully as a result and even though you may not need the help, we all do occasionally make mistakes, or there are better ways to say/do things. It helps them to feel better, too.
>
> **Be kind, supportive, encouraging** – these go much, much further than nagging and getting upset.
>
>> I very, very rarely criticize someone for the things they do that irritate me, especially the little things, I just let them slide, and I almost always try to talk about the big things kindly, though sometimes my frustrations leak through – that is something I am still working on.
>
> **Pick up the pieces yourself** – sometimes it is far kinder, and much less aggravating to straighten out, clean up, etc. what is bothering you than to fret about it. [Hint: just don't get in their personal work space unless you ask.]

By all means **talk about it with them**. They will try to be neater, more organized; but don't expect miracles. It is not in their nature. Be willing to compromise.

Messy, free-spirited, creative types do cause angst for more organized types. **Understanding from both sides of the fence can help bridge these difficult gaps.** Probably the most important idea to reemphasize is that **'messy' types don't try to aggravate perfectionist types on purpose**. Whatever makes them the way they are is very difficult to change. I am a good example. I have tried for years and I just never quite get there, even at my best.

One thing that is positive and vastly different for the more free-spirited of us is that since we don't concern ourselves with details and 'excessive' organization we can rarely be accused of 'nit-picking' or perfectionist behaviors.

Got a nitpicker/perfectionist in your life? Brainstorm how your next session will go with them. How you feel, what you think about, how you will react. Can you get creative and come up with a unique positive approach that makes them notice that you have changed how you will do business with them?

Got a free-spirited, messy type in your life? Ditto the paragraph above.

Critical/Derogatory, Put-down, One-uppers, Invalidates Others Behaviors

Some people really do put other people down. Sometimes it is obvious – as if they could care less about your feelings; at other times it can be a bit fuzzy in the interpretation, but you certainly end up feeling bad. Most of us ARE hurt by this type of behavior and negativity. The 'I am not good enough' feelings come boiling up and we have to struggle to regain our self-control and our self-worth.

Some Key Ideas

Many times, the 'perpetrator' may not see their statement(s) as derogatory, especially if there is indeed a gray area for interpretation. **We all see things differently – what you find hurtful may seem like a neutral statement of fact to them.** This goes back to a key idea in the first chapter: **most difficult people don't have a clue about how they are coming across to others** – even really negative, rude, obnoxious put-er-downers. They don't know the emotional havoc they cause. It can be very hard to accept this, but it is often true.

Try not to show outward signs of upset. This can be very hard. Take time to feel and think about how you feel after the interaction so you don't stuff all of this.

Ask for clarification: whether the remark is blatantly derogatory to being subtly so, **you have a right to understand it**, to understand why it was said, and to understand more about the person who said it, i.e. their motivation, their concern with you, etc. Make sure to phrase this and say it neutrally, without rancor, e.g. sk as kindly as possible. Yes, that can be very difficult because our hot buttons may have been pushed and our self-worth seriously challenged.

> "Paul, I am not sure I understood what you meant by that last remark. Could we get a cup of coffee and talk about what your concerns are?"

If the remark was made within a group/meeting/in public, its often best to let it ride until you can get the person alone. Document exactly what was said and the context and then approach them as soon as possible to seek understanding. Don't let these things fester!

Make sure you let them know, after they have had a chance to explain, how the remark made you feel.

> "You may not have meant it the way I took it, Paul, however I think you should know that what you said and the way you said it made me very upset. I felt like you were putting me down."

Always try to get in something akin to, "Thanks for the explanation, Paul. Please just ask me in the future if you have any concerns with me. I am always open to positive dialogue."

This is a GREAT tactic because:

> They won't expect you to remain calm and to ask for an explanation, so you will catch them by surprise.
>
> It is a means of regaining your own self-control.
>
> They will think twice about saying something to you again in the same way. However, be aware that they may take their tactics underground when thwarted in the open.
>
> You have an opportunity to deal with your own emotions by letting them know how this made you feel.
>
> You can often tell by their reaction whether they meant it or not, i.e. a true put-er-downer may be flustered by your reaction; someone else may be just confused at why you brought the whole thing up.

Keep in mind that often this type of behavior comes from a need to put others down so they can feel good. They have a very poor self-image and sense of worth. You can be kind because you are in-control and you do have self-worth.

Sometimes it is good to start an inner dialogue during and after these types of encounters:

> "Calm down."
>
> "You ARE 'good enough.'"
>
> "This is their stuff."
>
> "Stay positive; don't buy into their negativity."
>
> And so on

Always Right Behaviors

I had several people in my life for many years who were always right, literally. I can remember no time in which they ever apologized for anything or ever admitted they were wrong. Amazing.

You might think these types are the supreme egotists, but I am not sure the two always go hand in hand. I think this type of behavior is very much the result of a very poor self-image – to admit being wrong would make them look bad to themselves, and as they think, to others.

I have discussed at length the concept of 'being right' in several earlier sections of this book. My fundamental take is two-fold:

> **You can be right and be kind at the same time.**
>
> **What is so important about being right?**

Always ask yourself that second question when dealing with an 'always right' person. If you can let them be right without really giving up anything except your ego, let them be right. Who cares?

If you are truly vested in being right, there are always kind ways to do that and there are almost always ways to draw the other person into your perspective:

> **Compromise**
>
> **Get them vested in your ideas, the problem, the solution**
>
> **Help them own part of the positive outcome**
>
> **Add some of their thoughts and ideas to your own**
>
>> (If we really listen, this can be beneficial not only to them and their ego, but to our work as well.)

A last word: **being right is hardly ever worth all the frustration, choose kindness instead**. (Dyer/Koob)

Self-centered/Egotist, Narcissistic, Self-absorbed, Know-it-all Behaviors

> "The dysfunctional behavior you see on the outside is a reflection
>
> of the insecurity present on the inside." (Crowe)

NOTE: This is probably true of most difficult behaviors.

Yes, there are really egotistical people. Most of the time the only way they affect me today, unless they are otherwise being negative, is to amuse me and to make me sad at the same time.

You have gained so much insight throughout this book that you probably know what is about to follow, and not much more actually needs to be said:

> Stay true to yourself and these types have no power over us.
>
> If you need to, and you are alone or with someone you can trust implicitly, go ahead and vent a bit, because they can get under our skin occasionally. They can just seem to be a bit too much to take at times.

Above all -- **Be yourself**; center yourself in your values and qualities. Bring this you to the table at all times when dealing with difficult people.

Be kind, too. because they are in a much different space than you are. You can afford to be kind because you are in-control.

Questions and Ideas for Contemplation

Keep in mind: almost all difficult behaviors are rooted in a poor sense of self-worth. Anytime we spend in positive contact with a colleague by paying attention to them, and by acknowledging, appreciating, and recognizing who they are and what they do, adds to the possibilities of success exponentially. It also adds to our own humanity.

People who are deeply vested in things being absolutely perfect and who put themselves, or seem to put themselves above others, really have a tremendous amount of inner negative stuff they are dealing with. We can always rise up within our own self-worth and humanity to understand that we may be able to make a positive difference in their lives if we maintain our own self-control. Yes, it can be tough, because these types are terrific button-pushers and they often don't seem to care about how we feel. Still our greatest strength is staying within our core values and qualities and not letting them 'get to us.'

It does take some practice and often a fair amount of time to deal with some of the feelings that bubble up when we have to deal with these behaviors. Be patient with yourself, take care of yourself, be kind to yourself.

Chapter 18

Really Negative Behaviors

Negative Behaviors

These are behaviors that very often accompany or are 'melded' with other behaviors. All of the suggestions we have made to this point apply to working with negativity.

A really negative person can have a major impact on the overall aura of a team of people... but so can a very positive person. From my experience, positivity will win hands down if there is no giving in to the negativity.

So, my first piece of advice is really basic:

Be as positive a force as you can for yourself and for your team.

I am not a naturally outgoing, bubbly positive person. I am fundamentally shy. I have to work at letting my good feelings out into the world. I do that best by writing. However, I have made a concerted effort over the last few years to bring my inner positivity out more in my everyday interactions with people. I find it easy to do in settings where I am working with people, not so easy when I am out there in public. Interestingly, I am energetic and positive when I give seminars. That is where that part of me really comes out.

We are all different in this respect. Some people are naturally out-going; some are very shy and controlled. Most of us are, like me, somewhere in-between. No matter! Positivity shows in how you approach life in general: by the choices you make., how you talk to others, how you hold yourself, and especially how you respond in various situations.

I have seen positivity work remarkable miracles on a team. One truly cheerful person can blow negativity right out the window. Do what you can within the scope of your basic personality. Even if you are basically shy like me, you can make a difference. Make an effort to spread positivity wherever you go and with everyone you interact with, especially those negative types. It is amazing what an effect you can have over time. We can all be positive – just pick the approach to use by how you feel.

Key Ideas

Let the negativist know you plan to stay positive regardless of their attitude:

> "Yes, Mary, we have some problems here, but I am willing to do what I can. I really believe we can make a difference if we try. Do you want to have lunch and talk about it? I will buy."

> She probably won't want to go with you, even with the free lunch offer. She might prefer to whine, complain, and blame. It is how she gets attention. Keep trying. **Positive attention** can win out in the long run.

Coming back with a **solution-minded approach** can help change their dynamics with you over time. On rare occasions they may even decide to buy into your suggestions:

> "Ned, you have some real concerns that need to be addressed by the team. Why don't we form a small committee – you, me, and Alice, as she seems interested in some of these issues, too. We will brainstorm some ideas for making things better and take them to the boss."

> Don't expect them to do this either; it sounds like too much effort to a doomsayer. However, they may stop their constant complaining to and around you after a few responses like this from you. You are no fun anymore.

Don't listen to their negativity for long and don't buy into anything they say. If they are inveterate nay-sayers and gloom spreaders, this is probably how they gain attention. If you give them that attention, they will keep you on their list of people to bother on a regular basis.

They want and desperately **need attention, give them positive attention**. Whenever (if ever) they come out with something positive, or do something for you or the team, make sure you jump on that with **acknowledgment, appreciation, and recognition. Don't let any opportunity pass to pay positive attention to them!**

These behavioral types like to have their little cliques of mutual 'doomists.' Form your own group, in a sense, through your positive interactions with the rest of the members of your team. As your positivity and fun leaks out to the negative clique(s), you will likely start drawing some of them away. Positivity is much more fun than negativity.

Don't take what they say to heart. Negative people can be very critical, pushy, demanding, egotistical, etc. They have oodles of stuff they are dealing with and you don't have to accept any of it. Try **to maintain your self-worth, dignity, and self-control**. After a short period of time, they will realize you literally can't be bothered by their negativity.

Renew yourself. If you have a real negativist in your group, they can drain even the best of us at times, particularly when we are being hit by other things: overwork, illness, not enough sleep, etc. If you find yourself getting down, even a little, take a break, read a short positive saying/passage. [Keep a book of sayings; or motivation verses near to hand.] Have a brief positive interaction with a friend, call home and say hi to your wife, kids, or just take a moment and look at a picture you have of your loved ones or of a special place.

You can even be brave and talk to them about their negativity, kindly:

> "Ralph, you seem like a really intelligent guy, but you always seem so unhappy. Is there anything I can do to help? It is really important that we try to keep everyone's attitude as positive as possible around here. I think you could help a lot. I know when you say nice things to me, it makes a big difference to my day.

You can say this even if he's never said anything nice to you. He probably doesn't see himself as being negative.

You are bringing up his overall mood and how you see it. You are giving him a tweak in the right direction; by suggesting he could make a difference adding some positivity, which also speaks to his ego. And you are offering your support. It is not unusual for people to try to be the way you want them to be if they know what that is.

You CAN make a difference.

I have written about this a number of times in various works, but in general the idea is this:

> How we interact with others and the world can be positive, neutral, or negative. When we add positivity to the mix, we really do have a chance of affecting someone's day for the better (or there week, month, or even their life!).

Whiners, Complainers, Blamers, Moody Behaviors

I have had remarkable success over the past few years with these types of behaviors, especially since beginning difficultpeople.org and working on all these ideas for being successful with difficult people. I use the techniques above, but more than anything I focus on two things:

> **Finding ways to be more positive myself**
>
> **Being open, honest, direct, and kind** with them about their behaviors.

Say it!

> Stephanie, I really like you a lot, but It is so hard for me to see your positive side when you are so often whining or worrying about things. Take it from me, this really doesn't do you, or anyone, any good. Can we sit down and hash out all these problems and concerns. I know we can make a difference on some things; and when we can't make a difference directly, I will bet there are other things we can do."

Worrying, whining, complaining, and blaming people won't stop this bad habit because you bring it up once. You have to maintain your positivity and bring it up regularly. They will likely start to change. In essence, you are helping them begin to pay attention to themselves -- the key to developing a positive self-worth.

"Complaining," a special case

Complainers like to sound off about almost anything and everything, **until**, and this technique works quite well, you 'push' them to **seeking solutions**. They will either back off the complaining around you, or buy into actually doing something about what they are yapping about.

> "Ted, that is a legitimate concern. Why don't you write it up, delineate what you think is the problem, and suggest several solutions? I will ask the boss to put it on the team agenda for our next meeting."

You can go so far as to bring it up at the next meeting, even if Ted backs away from your suggestion and any responsibility for a solution. "Ted brought up a concern that I think we all can work on..."

Many complainers just seem to like to complain. When you stop them in their tracks with positive suggestions, it is very likely they will get very tired of your in-control, open approach and either find another outlet, switch behaviors (possible), or give it up because they aren't getting the attention they want.

Don't forget, giving difficult people positive attention is one of the **Key** ways to begin effect change.

"Blamers," a really special case

Blamers take the art of negativity to greater heights; they dump everything, and I mean everything, onto others' shoulders. [Hint: Gossipers are usually blamers, too.] Whining, complaining, moodiness, and blaming frequently go hand in hand in the same person's repertoire. Unfortunately, you or someone else on the team shoulders this person's negative view of the world.

Blamers don't accept responsibility for their own work or life.

You have a right and obligation to stand up for yourself and others. **Never ignore a blamer; never agree with them; always use an assertive, kind stance to deal with them**:

> "Ursula, I don't feel what you just said is accurate about Ben. Are you willing to talk with him about this concern? I really don't want you to be misunderstood, because it might look bad for you."

Blamers will almost always back down if they are challenged; and after a few challenges, you can be pretty well assured they will avoid saying anything around you ever again.

If you have a good rapport with others in your group, help them become aware of this technique. You never have to be nasty or negative yourself – **remain calm and poised, state the facts, bring it into the open, suggest a dialogue.**

Moodiness

We are all moody at times – some people are moodier than others. Gently and kindly **inquiring** about a coworker's moodiness can help. **Don't push; let them seek their own solutions.** Your best tools are your own positivity and your willingness to pay them some attention and **offer support**. Sometimes all a moody person needs is some **kindness**, and to **feel like someone else cares**.

Moody people are not necessarily depressed or even 'down.' When I was younger, people often thought I was really moody, down, depressed, etc. Truth was, I was often just thinking about things – I would shut myself off from everything around me and not even notice people saying "Hi" to me when I passed, etc. When a friend and I talked about this, it opened my eyes a good bit. I am still shy, introverted, and often spend time contemplating things, but I try to be more receptive and responsive to everyone now. So, a moody person may just need a heads up!

When we can maintain our own self-worth and positivity, these behaviors can be some of the easiest to be successful with. They can also be emotional and psychologically draining, so stay on top of how you are feeling, too.

Some negativists will never change their stripes, but we can make a difference in how they interact with us, and often within the team. We can't always make a difference in how they interact with the rest of the world or their overall attitude and demeanor.

Stay positive, do what you CAN do.

Rude/Abrupt, Boorish, Obnoxious Behaviors

"Well, Excu-u-u-s-s-e me!"

Remember Steve Martin's 'schtick'? This is probably the nicest response you would actually like to give the rude, boorish, obnoxious person in your life. You could probably think of a few more choice words, too.

I have seen quite a bit in my life and work, but I am not sure whether these types have never learned the niceties of human interactions, whether they enjoy being rude and obnoxious, or whether they just **don't have a clue how they are coming across**. From my experience, however, it seems to be the latter.

Hard as that may be to believe, I have known some really obnoxious people, and I don't think they did know how they came across. One remains in my mind and psyche as an outstanding example of someone who was incredibly boorish and yet he truly thought he was a devoutly religious man and a nice guy, overall. Everybody else thought something else entirely.

Your best strategy

They are not going to find out how they come across to others unless someone tells them. They are not going to know how they affect you unless you tell them. Both these are things you can and should do. Just find the kindest way to do it:

> "Vick, you have some terrific ideas and I think the rest of the team really needs to hear them. I think I should let you know, though, that the way you present things is sometimes pretty caustic and you tend to turn people off. If you stay calm and cool, like I've seen you do with Mr. Baumgartner, you will have everyone's attention."

Get a compliment in there; it is worth its weight in gold. And it helps a lot to give people a vision of what is acceptable. **Imagery can be a very effective tool.**

> "Terry, I would sincerely appreciate it if you could present things in a calm, controlled, and kinder manner. You might be surprised at how well received your ideas will be, then. I think you may end up having much less resistance in our meetings."

> "Elsie, you are such a lovely person, please talk to me calmly and nicely. I will pay attention, I promise."

You are giving them good reasons to change their ways; you will just have to see if they bite. They very well may take the bait. Keep working with this idea for more permanent change.

Be sure to compliment them if they make an effort to change; and support them in their efforts, trials, and tribulations as they will probably relapse into old habits at times and make some mistakes.

There is that **positivity** thing, too: positivity does rub off if you stick to your guns. Keep at it!

I might even use **humor** with an obnoxious type. But use CAUTION, please. Humor can backfire, and you should only use it if you feel confident it won't offend. Part of this depends on how your overall relationship is with this person; if it is strained and has been for some time, humor probably is not a good idea. As an example:

> "Whoa, there Cowboy, I think you have a bit too much grease in the skillet. How about running that last part by me and leaving out the irritating bits? I am listening partner, and I want to like what I hear."

There is also a story I heard or read, which goes something like this,

> A baggage claim customer service representative was trying to help a very disgruntled passenger whose luggage had gotten lost. He was being extremely rude and belligerent. Finally, the exasperated representative., trying her best to remain calm and friendly, said, "Sir, there are only two people in the world who care where your bag is, and one of them is rapidly losing interest." He calmed immediately and apologized for his behavior.

Doomsayers and Curmudgeons

Just a word or two about those folks who just seem to like to spread negativity and ill-will at every turn. All information in the previous chapter is applicable here.

Two keys:

> First: **Maintain your own positivity** in spite of their doom, gloom, and grumpiness. Find every opportunity to be positive to/with them: smile, compliment them on a regular basis:
>
>> "Mildred, I love your new dress."
>>
>> "I heard you shot an 185 at league last week, Edgar, great job!"
>
> Don't expect a positive response; at least not the first 100 times. These types are typically well-entrenched in their behavior. You may be pleasantly surprised though that they will eventually start coming around.
>
> **DON'T join in/buy in to their negativity**; or add to the complaining, blaming, worrying, etc. that they are so good at. You are better than this. If all else fails, leave. They will eventually get the point.

These types may be very hard to effect change with. Your positive efforts, however, may have a positive effect over time. Keep at it, and bring others into the effort as well.

Stubborn/Hard-headed, Selfish

[See *Obstructionist*' and *'No' behaviors* in Chapter 12. That information is also relevant here.)

The truth is most of us are stubborn when someone pushes us in a direction we don't want to go. A major part of being successful with a stubborn or selfish person is to **get them to talk**. The better you **listen** and **understand** what they **need, want, and desire**; and the more you can give them a sense that **they have been heard,** and that their ideas are important and will be considered, the more likely they will come out of that hard shell and be willing to give a little.

Invest yourself in who they are and then invest them in a broader perspective one step at a time. They may not want to listen to you the first few times you spend time listening to them, but they will eventually come around. Be patient, and use your best communication skills to draw them out and to eventually open the door so you and others can be heard.

A true story, really!

I once worked with a guy who pretty much has every quality discussed in the last two chapters and then some. He was rude, obnoxious, put people down to elevate himself, was extremely rigid in his thinking, and was rarely happy with anyone else's work. As I look back at those days, now some years in my past, I think of the good things I did in dealing with him, and I really think about the things I could have done better. I am not sure whether I could have ever changed the guy. He was so tremendously insecure that he had built up all these behaviors as defense mechanisms. But I do think I could have made more of a difference with him if I had all this knowledge and these skills back then that I have now. I think that I could have affected his relationship with me and with other people on our team much more positively.

Questions and Ideas for Contemplation

I often go back in my mind to different problem people I dealt with throughout my life and replay those relationships. It helps me consider what I would do if those types of concerns were presented to me today. I can learn a great deal from working through things I did, and things I could have done better. This is a great exercise to consider as you continue to develop your knowledge and skills.

Chapter 19
'The world is out to get me,' Behaviors

These are also behaviors that are often associated with other difficult behaviors discussed throughout this book. They are rooted in mistrust, fear, and insecurity.

Suspicious, Distrusting, Paranoid/fearful Behaviors
Trust

The most critical element to building or rebuilding a relationship with an individual who is highly suspicious and fearful is trust. It is the foundation for everything else I will discuss in this chapter and it is an important factor in all relationships – allow me to repeat that:

ALL RELATIONSHIPS

require

TRUST

... if they are to be productive and collegial.

Keys to developing trust

Trust is tremendously affected by people's experiences. Untrusting relationships a person may have had with other people and in other difficult situations (especially during major life and work changes) can affect them for some time. For some it is easy to trust an open, honorable person; for others, trust takes considerable effort and time to develop.

It starts with YOU

Trust and **respect** others: You can be a catalyst for a trusting relationship with a given person and within your team. You can hope it will naturally work the other way, because you ARE trustworthy, but it probably won't, not for everyone.

Appreciate and recognize others

Openly and regularly appreciating others is plain good sense. When we appreciate and recognize other people, they notice. It is perhaps the most fundamental need of people in a work environment (and in life!). **We all want to feel needed and useful.** It is great when we are recognized by our colleagues and other significant people in our lives.

Care: people want to feel cared for. It doesn't have to be 'touchy/feely'; it has to do with **respectful attention**, and can be as simple as remembering details about them and what is important to them. A sense that you **care** about them and their concerns goes a long way.

Connectedness: being **available** when they ask for help or seek friendship is very important. You don't have to be at their beck and call, and it doesn't have to take a great deal of time. Let them know what you are capable of giving. Small things, like stopping by in the morning to say hello, inviting them to coffee once in a while, or accepting their invitation for a brief chat can all make a difference.

Being yourself: People recognize when someone is not being honest and open. Mistrustful people are especially sensitive to this. Just be yourself; and be willing to share who you are and what you are about openly and honestly.

Open and Honest

Being open and honest doesn't necessarily mean you share intimate secrets with a colleague. It means when push comes to shove you can let them know how you feel about something at work, and it means you are willing to listen to how they feel. It is about sharing what is important to colleagues who need to exchange information, ideas, and feelings in order to be successful at what they do.

Developing this type of relationship is what needs to happen in order to be successful with mistrustful people. It starts with you and it can take some time. Be patient and persevere.

Phobic, Anxious

Many of us have minor phobias and things that make us anxious. With some people this can be fairly disruptive in their life and in their work-life. Phobias are not necessarily things like 'spiders' or 'heights'. We can be afraid of many things, e.g. answering the phone, which certainly could be a major concern in a work environment.

There is a very gray area between a phobia as such and something that typically causes us considerable and regular anxiety. You cannot help/save/cure anxious people by solving their fears and phobias. Unless you are professionally qualified, you should never attempt to diagnose someone or make recommendations regarding taking medications or other substances for anxiety. You and your business could get in serious trouble.

You can help them by following many of the positive guidelines outlined in this book:

> **Be positive**
>
> **Pay them positive attention**
>
> **Recognize them for accomplishments**
>
> **Thank them**
>
> **Appreciate them for who they are**
>
> **Acknowledge them often**
>
> **Offer to be supportive and helpful if they need it**

Their anxiety may not go away, but it will be greatly tempered by your positivity.

Overly emotional, Constantly needs Attention

These two behaviors go back to several we discussed earlier in Chapter 13: Sycophant, Overly reliant, Co-dependent, Clingy, etc. Please review this section for more insight.

I have put this issue back on the agenda at this point because it is important to reemphasize one very basic point that keeps weaving its way into this discussion: **people often crave and desperately need attention**. Often, we spend our work time so focused on what we are doing and trying to accomplish that we forget there are human beings all around us with many mixed emotions and mixed emotional baggage. Sometimes this can reach such a point that we feel like no one even knows we exist. Everything is so automated and technically focused, we may not know the person's name in a cubicle three spaces down.

This is a BIG leadership skill, but it is very useful to all of us in the trenches, too:

Get out and about and contact people.

It is a great break for you; **it supports others immeasurably**, it really doesn't take that much time, and heck, you even get some exercise in the bargain.

What do you lose? Yes, maybe It is fifteen minutes of your day that you could be slaving over another form or something, but from personal experience, if I get up every so often and take a stroll, I am much more likely to stay focused and accomplish more when I get back at it.

Take time for people, please. You may feel emotionally drained sometimes by the effort to be with a dependent, needy colleague; but in the long run you will develop your own techniques and style and it will energize you, rather than drain you. **You are helping someone and that is one of the greatest gifts you can give in life.**

Emotional and Attention needing people may just need a bit of recognition and support. You can give that: through regular positive contact, through a quick morning e-mail, through a "Hi Yah" as you pass by; and in a myriad of other ways. Isn't it worth it when you get a smile in return? Think about it – think about this every day.

Question and Ideas for Contemplation

Some difficult people ARE difficult to help, but many just need a bi of an effort from someone to pay positive attention to them. YOU can be that person, without really that much effort.

Yes, there are really difficult people who don't respond positively to much. They may even be a lost cause. Isn't it worth it to make an effort? It speaks to who you are. It says a good bit about your humanity. Speak loudly!

Chapter 20

'Out there,' Behaviors

Bizarre, Odd, Weird

We all have our little quirks. They are our unique way of interacting with the world. One of mine is I can be pretty 'goofy' when I am with people I know, and sometimes just for the heck of it. It is my way of staying relaxed, not taking things too seriously, and adding a little fun to the world.

The problem with behaviors that strike us as a bit odd is that they can be taken the wrong way.

> **di gustibus non est disputandum**
> **In taste there is no disputing**

Unfortunately, little 'quirks' can be greatly exacerbated if the person manifests a difficult behavior to start with. When we add odd behaviors to the mix, we start to question a person's mental and emotional fitness.

Tolerance and Learning

One key to understanding another person's unusual habits and strange doings is to be strong enough to tolerate differences, even those odd differences that may bother us a bit.

Another key is to jump off from our willingness to tolerate differences to learn about the other person and the interesting way in which they approach the world. We can learn more about ourselves in the process, too.

Bizarre

Yes, there are some people who exhibit rather bizarre behaviors. Still, we can give them the benefit of the doubt and reserve judgment until we understand more. If the behavior(s) is generally disruptive or causes concern in your group and its mission, then certainly it may be worth broaching with the person. We can do this as we have approached all concerns in this book:

> **Kindly**
>
> **Openly** – with understanding, concern, and **without judgment**
>
> **Support and an offer to help**
>
> By using excellent communication skills that begin with a **willingness to listen carefully**

It may also be important to bring this out in the open with fellow team members, because anything that is rumor bred and rumor-mill exaggerated can quickly dissolve into cliquish innuendo and unfair judgments.

Judging others

We judge others far more than we realize. Even if we only do it in our minds, we make judgments every day.

Sometimes these are obvious statements reflecting what we are perceiving:

"She's fat."

"He's ugly."

"That is a dumb thing to have done."

"What is with that weird way he walks?"

And so on.

They are still unkind. If we **learn to pay attention to our thoughts**, we can learn to **lessen our tendency to make negative judgments of others** or even turn our judgments around:

"I am concerned about Martha's health; she's put on so much weight. Do you think there is a way we can help her, without hurting her feelings?" There very well might be. But always be kind and supportive.

"I should help John with that, he doesn't seem to have the knack yet. I'll see if he wants some assistance."

Sometimes our inner statements are suppositions with little basis, until we know more:

"Alice can't do anything right."

"Bob is such an idiot; he's probably out there screwing up the Benson project right now."

"Ellie just isn't going to get it done on time, and I am going to get in trouble."

"That is a really strange way to do that. Just shows you what a nutcase Ben is."

Watch yourself very carefully for two or three days and see how many, type, and the degree of judgments you make in your mind in the course of a day. **Negativity breeds Negativity**. We all can do better. I catch myself everyday making judgments that I don't need to make and that serve no one for the better. I know I can do better: **Positivity breeds Positivity!**

Really Odd and Bizarre behaviors

Behaviors that may be threatening to you, members of your group, or to the person who is exhibiting them should be brought up to someone in authority, i.e. if someone seems suicidal or is acting much more strangely than normal, there may be a serious concern that needs to be addressed immediately.

Don't ever take chances with your safety or the safety of others,

including the person exhibiting the behavior.

Remember, you may be the person who stops a suicide, a shooting, or some other bad event. Today we have to be conscious of these types of possibilities and make sure that appropriate authorities are notified. It IS better to be safe, than sorry.

Please Keep in Mind

Oddities we see in another person's behavior can be the result of a wide variety of factors that we may know nothing about or don't understand fully.

Physical conditions beyond their control, which may or may not be related to an emotional/psychological issue

> If you consider such behavior dangerous on concerning please report it to someone in authority.

Individual and personal quirks (Including ways in which we relate to the world around us that have served us in the past.)

> These can easily be blown way out of proportion if the person is otherwise a negative, disruptive force in the workplace

Cultural, Ethnic, Religious differences can affect different people in various ways. You can always ask to help you understand them, so that you understand how they feel and think about their own behavior. And, be kind; seek understanding if it is important to you; be tolerant.

They are a child of this universe, too.

They are in their own space and dealing with it the best they can for this moment in time. We can always choose how we respond to/with them. We can always choose to be negative or to be positive.

Questions and Ideas for Contemplation

One thing we often forget to think about when dealing with others, especially behaviors that are really difficult to deal with or difficult to understand, is that **we can always ask**. There are many examples throughout this book of ways to approach people in a kind, positive way.

If you take the time to think things through, you can find a way to deal with a difficult situation in a like manner. Isn't that so much better than any negative-laden alternatives?

Chapter 21
'There are laws against these' Behaviors

Sexual Innuendo, Advances, Inappropriate Comments or Suggestions, Flirtatious, Seductive, Harassing Behaviors
Know your Organization's policies

If you have concerns about any type of inappropriate behavior, you should read through the policies published by your business very carefully. If you do not know where to find them, check with Human Resources. **It is very important to know how these issues are expected to be handled and what options you have** when you feel that your concerns have reached a point where you want and/or need support and assistance. If you have any doubts as to the proper procedures, the meaning of a guideline or policy, or what you should do next, contact a Human Resources professional and sit down and discuss your options.

IMPORTANT: many companies address these issues in their employee handbooks. Use these types of documents as a reference point for further understanding and action. Regulations may dictate how you should respond to inappropriate behavior/actions of your boss. It is important to read these documents thoroughly and to take appropriate action. Fundamentally how you approach these concerns will be your decision.

As a manager I have had to deal with some pretty serious concerns in the workplace. Any type of sexual inappropriateness cannot be tolerated. I have also seen this, as an employee, at work amongst team members. The fundamental perspective is:

> **If it is inappropriate to you, it is inappropriate.**

And it needs to be dealt with immediately.

But how?

Dealing with inappropriate behaviors

There are many issues that should be considered around what must be done when someone is approaching someone else in an inappropriate and sexual manner.

- Legal issues abound – on both sides of the coin
- It can be very difficult to prove
- People are going to go through a tremendous amount of angst and pain
- It never seems like there can be a win - win situation

This IS a personal decision and you must decide whether to take this issue to an appropriate agency at your place of work, hire legal assistance, request mediation, etc. Make sure you are comfortable with the decision you make to go forward. Only you can make this decision. **Err on the side of caution and get assistance**

if you have any doubts. Mediation is always an option for these issues and often a wise choice even if you want to try to resolve the concern personally

General considerations that can help

First: if you feel someone is approaching you inappropriately, let them know how you feel.

Do this as soon as you feel uncomfortable with what is going on. The sooner you let them know you are not happy with this type of attention the better.

Do it in as kind and understanding a way as possible, even if they are being obnoxious and crude.

Be firm and assertive. Don't back down. Let them know that you won't tolerate this type of behavior.

> "Kelly, I need to let you know that I am very uncomfortable with the statements you have been making toward me. I feel they are very inappropriate. I would appreciate it if you would stop."

Regardless of what they say – denial, laugh-it-off, etc., stick to your guns.

> "Kelly, I am very serious about this. I don't want to have to report this, but I will if it continues."

IMPORTANT: **Document** every incident and every interaction, be specific and comprehensive. If anyone witnesses the behavior, try to get them to sign your notes or make a statement that you can file, too.

Second: if the behavior doesn't stop, make one more attempt to reason with them. This will give you at least two specific incidents where you have documented your response to their inappropriateness and your request for them to terminate it.

> "Kelly, I asked you to please stop this sexual innuendo and what I feel are inappropriate and crude actions. If you continue, I will take this immediately to the authorities. I have documented and dated everything you have said and done and my requests for you to stop."

Third: If the behavior has escalated, or if it continues after several attempts to curtail it, go to your immediate superior and tell him/her. Be sure you let them know that you have documentation of the inappropriate behaviors of your colleague, as well as your responses. Also make sure he/she understands that you are documenting this meeting with him/her.

It is probably a good idea to keep this information far from prying eyes – under lock and key, encrypted, or protected by a password.

You may also want to store a copy of this material with a very close and trusted friend who is not a colleague.

Finally: If the behavior has not stopped and your boss does not seem willing to pursue this issue, take it to other appropriate resources.

> Human Resources or other applicable office at work – they can point you in the right direction and should be able to suggest ways to deal with it.

If you feel it is necessary, get a lawyer. You may wish to do this earlier in the process so that you have guidance and support. Get the help and support you need. Keep in mind the law is on your side, but avoiding legal hassles will save you considerable anxiety if it is at all possible to resolve the concern in any other acceptable way for you.

At this point, it is wise to make sure that there is follow-up. Don't let any significant period of time go without something being done. This is your life and work, you are uncomfortable, and **legally you have the right to work in an environment that is free from harassment.**

Take care of yourself

This type of concern can very difficult, even devastating. Do everything you can to support yourself and to **have people you can turn to for support**. You shouldn't feel guilty or blame yourself for this, though you may. You are a child of the universe and deserve to be treated kindly and honorably. Support from a qualified professional may also be very helpful in working through these types of concerns: counselor, personal coach, minister, etc.

Questions and Ideas for Contemplation

In all my experiences as a manager, I have never had a situation like this escalate beyond the initial three phases above. I think this is because I dealt with it quickly and firmly. This can save everyone a tremendous amount of angst and turmoil.

Many inappropriate suggestions and actions (up to a point) are 'in fun,' or so the perpetrator says. **Obviously, they are not fun for the recipient.** However, the perpetrator will often immediately back-peddle, apologize, and cease and desist when they are confronted. Make the choices that are best for you. You should **never** have to put up with this type of behavior.

Chapter 22

Succeeding with REALLY Difficult Coworkers

You can consider any of the many types of behaviors discussed in this book and imagine a person who takes these to extremes:

> A very volatile coworker who explodes on a regular basis
>
> An extremely negative colleague who can't ever say anything positive about anyone or anything; and who complains, whines, and blames at every opportunity, to whomever will listen.
>
> A paranoid team member who secrets himself in his cubicle and never interacts with anyone, even avoiding team meetings they are afraid to attend because of 'what might happen'.
>
> A person who creates utter havoc amongst team members by spreading lies and rumors on a daily basis.
>
> And so on.

How can we deal with REALLY difficult coworkers and be successful?

First

Even really difficult people respond to **kindness, attentiveness, understanding, positivity, honesty, appreciation, acknowledgment, and recognition. Be patient and work hard** at this. It really can be worth the effort. You will also learn a great deal about life and yourself in the bargain.

It can be rewarding for you and for the person you are being kind to. I have seen this happen with very difficult people both in my own interactions with them and through the kindness and positivity of others.

Remember it is important to always **take care of yourself and be safe**!

Also, remember that your goal is a positive working situation for you and others. You are not out to save someone else or to change who they are so they are more like you. Give them space to be themselves and to learn that positivity is simply a better choice they can make.

Second

You should consider the possibility that if a person's behavior is extreme, that there may be psychological, emotional, mental, and/or physical reasons for what is being manifested. You can't make them go get a check-up, but you can **ask them about their well-being**. Part of what you can do and say depends on your relationship with them. If you have made an effort and been able to establish at least some positive interaction, you could probably suggest some help.

> "Gina, I am really worried about you. Is there anything I can do to help? Are you okay?"

If Gina takes the hint and opens up a little, then you may be able to suggest something. Be cautious and supportive; this can be a very sensitive area. It is best to leave this alone unless you have established a supportive relationship and do care about how they are doing.

You might even be able to slip in a "Have you been to a doctor lately?" depending on how it would be taken. Be kind and caring in your approach.

You can keep trying

All of the suggestions, ideas, skills, and tools in this book may also work with very difficult behaviors/people. Review recommendations for working with specific behaviors. Make sure you delineate the concerns you have with their behavior; and practice and use recommended skills and tools. If they work, it will take time. Be patient, but also make sure you are taking care of yourself. NEVER place yourself or anyone else at risk. You can only do so much.

Caution! Drug and alcohol usage can greatly exacerbate difficult situations. If this is an obvious concern you will probably want to raise this issue with an authority figure or appropriate department.

These ideas and tools CAN work with even really difficult people. However, if serious mental, emotional, or physical concerns exist, or if in spite of your positive efforts your interactions and concerns with this person are still unresolved, then you should consider other alternatives.

See the next chapter – your positive influence throughout the workplace can have a significant effect even with really difficult people.

Some people may not respond to your efforts

Sometimes people are beyond our help. I have encountered extremely negative people, people with a large chip on their shoulder, people who have such low self-esteem that they can't seem to ever see the positive side of things, and people who are so defensive because of past hurts that they are beyond our humble efforts to help. Thankfully there are not many of these types. Many, many people do respond to positivity and kindness.

You can keep trying; or you can consider other possibilities. Some choices you can consider:

>If the concern is very serious, you may want to discuss with a supervisor. Make sure you have all your ducks in a row, document incidents, etc., and be as kind as possible in presenting your concerns. Remember the person you are concerned with may have serious physical, mental, or emotional concerns that should be addressed by a professional. It is not your place to make a diagnosis or even suggest this to a superior, except in a caring, concerned way.

>If the person you are concerned with is causing you significant grief, and you do not feel comfortable or safe remaining where you are, you can look for a new position or new job. You safety and mental health, as well as your families welfare, are more important than continuing to deal with a situation that is beyond your control.

Taking this to the next level

If you feel you have made every effort to be a positive, kind force in working with this individual and the negativity persists unrelentingly, bring it up with the boss. If you have documented your concerns and specific incidents, and if this person's pervasive difficult behavior is also affecting others, you will have the 'ammo' you need.

Sometimes it is one of the best choices you have left if you want to make a difference in your work space and if this person is creating an uncomfortable situation for all.

Be sure that your boss understands the seriousness of your concern, knows about, in detail, what you have done to try to help the situation and to help your colleague. Be clear that you want something done for the sake of your own work, the productivity and effectiveness of the team, and for this troubled colleague.

My outlook on life is always: if I am not having 'fun,' I need to do something. I try to take responsibility for my own life, and I when things are 'not fun,' I do something to change the situation. If it involves other people, I try to make changes as kindly and understandingly as possible.

If your boss will not or cannot do something, then you need to take this to Human Resources or another appropriate department in your organization.

Moving on

You always have choices. Sometimes they are tough choices to make. Weigh the possibilities and issues and move ahead. Wishing won't get you far. Doing something positive for you and others will. Here are some possible considerations:

> Continue to use your positive self in dealing with this person and the issues he/she raises.

>> It really is amazing what positivity can do.

> Consider changing locations within your building to move further away from this negativity.

>> It doesn't hurt to ask if this may be feasible.

> Consider changing jobs within the organization.

> Consider seeking a new job.

>> I have found that sometimes a negative situation is just the push I needed to get my life moving again. I have made major changes as the result of very poor work situations and been much happier and productive as a result. I have also learned a tremendous amount in the process.

You always have choices: choose wisely for YOU!

Important

If you have to make the judgment call on dealing with a really difficult individual. Ask yourself these questions:

> Have I done everything I can?
>
> Have I remained a positive, kind force in all my dealings with this person?
>
> Can I see any other recourse?

Then, if you feel you have done your best, take care of yourself and move ahead with your work and life.

Questions and Ideas for Contemplation

Do you have a REALLY difficult person at work? Delineate your concerns; it always helps to get down on paper all that is bothering you. Make sure you make an effort to understand the person and the behaviors that they are using. Understanding yourself and understanding them puts you in the best possible situation to help yourself, help them, and to make wise choices when you have to.

Chapter 23

Things You can do that Make a Difference

There are a great many suggestions in this book about the positive things you can do to improve your relationship and interactions with a difficult person. In addition, you can have a marked impact on the lives of your coworkers by the many small choices you make every day.

This doesn't have to be focused on any particular person. Do random acts of joy and kindness – everyone will be affected.

> Choose positivity – It is so much more fun than anything else.

The choices we make

Many of these I have done in my many roles as a leader, as an employee and team member, and as a person in this world. See the end of this chapter for a recent *Musing* I wrote that typifies my outlook on adding positivity to life.

Add some joy to the workplace every day

> **Compliment** your fellow coworkers
>
> **Pay all of them some positive attention** – you will all feel better
>
> Give a little gift – just because
>
> Kid around, have some fun, be a 'goofball,' so long as it is not at the expense of others
>
> Jazz up the place
>
>> Your space
>>
>> The bulletin board
>>
>> Rest rooms, lounge, hallways?
>>
>> Be creative, but also bear in mind everyone else and company rules and regulations. You may want to check with your boss first!
>
> Lend an ear – almost everyone likes to talk
>
> **Appreciate, Acknowledge, and Recognize your colleagues**
>
> **Recognize small wins; Acknowledge successes**
>
> **Appreciate team members** because they are important to your and your team's success
>
> You don't need a specific reason or event to appreciate someone: Just say, "**Thanks**," for being here.
>
> **Celebrate** birthdays, holidays, and other special events

> An e-mail or card (e-card) is great
>
> Give small gifts
>
> Take someone to lunch
>
> Go out of your way to thank people for things they do that impact you
>
>> E-mail
>>
>> Handwritten note for special help
>>
>> Phone call
>>
>> Walk over to their space and personally thank them. It can mean the world on a busy day.
>
> **Offer support and help** when you can. Even little things can make a difference to someone's day.
>
> **Be willing to listen** – sometimes a shoulder to lean on can help turn around a person's day.
>
> Get creative with positive ideas – it is fun and it makes a difference

The amazing truth

This all does make a difference and none of it takes much time, effort, energy, or money. On the contrary, it can influence better effectiveness, efficiency, and productivity. And it can add to your enjoyment and energy at work.

MUSINGS: 12/06/04

"A Little Chunk of Cheese"

A couple of night's ago, I talked my very busy and hard-working wife into going to a concert after work on a week night. Because she wanted to get as much done before leaving and because the concert was on her side of town, I agreed to meet her a few minutes before the concert in the parking lot. We also agreed to have dinner afterward.

She asked me to bring a chunk of cheese for her to nibble on before we went in, because we wouldn't be eating until quite late.

As the dutiful husband, I got the cheese out and some smoked sausage and cut off some generous slices and placed them in a plastic bag. I also cut a small chunk of cheese, took a major bite out of it, (leaving some terrific teeth marks, I might add), and placed it in another small plastic bag. Each of these two bags then were carefully placed in separate pockets of my coat.

When we finally linked up, I waited until she asked me if I had remembered the chunk of cheese (I tend to be forgetful). I nodded, stuck my hand in my pocket and produced the small, already partially devoured chunk.

> "Is this all you brought?" (My wife knows me pretty well, so she was already pretty sure this was some kind of joke, so she was half-smiling.)

Then I produced the second bag.

"You, goofball." Her smile widened. You are such a, goofball. (Etc.)."

What is the point of this little story?

It is so easy to add a bit of sparkle and joy to another's life. It doesn't take much effort. It is a great thing to do for them, especially when they have been working hard, and it is fulfilling to not only them, but you, too.

As you can tell I do this type of thing a lot. I have fun planning it and implementing it and watching what transpires as it unfolds. What is not to like?

We can add joy to life so easily – why not start today?

Make it part of who you are!

Questions and Ideas for Contemplation

You can come up with many more positive, uplifting ideas than are above. Brainstorm. THEN, make the effort to implement some of them.

"If you are not having fun, something's wrong."

(Koob, *A Perfect Day: Guide for a Better Life*)

You are the catalyst – make it happen.

Chapter 24
Taking Care of YOU

You can make more of a difference to others if you take care of yourself. You want to be at your best physically, emotionally, psychologically, mentally, and spiritually. Stay alert for signs of stress or other personal concerns.

Stress Management

The amazing thing about stress is we live with it day in and day out, we bring it home with us, and we even sleep with it. We've gotten so used to it, we rarely notice it any more unless it reaches a fever pitch or we have our first heart attack. DEAL WITH IT! Please.

There are lots of ideas for stress reduction. Pick from this list or find your own favorites. The important thing is to do something every day, preferably several times a day. It doesn't have to take much time.

TAKE A BREAK!

A short relaxing walk -- walking from one meeting to another or talking on your cell phone doesn't count. Go out of your way on your path to something else, or take a quick jaunt outside and around the building.

A two-minute meditative silence (five or ten if you really want to make a difference) is amazingly effective. Arrange for a short period of time for an undisturbed break (five minutes or so); meditate on something pleasurable. If you like more structure, take some classes and learn how, but a brief positive relaxation is what you are after.

> It really is amazing what a short period of quietude can do for you. Make it a habit.
>
> Take some deep breaths – I like to think of breathing out the bad stuff and breathing in the good. Powerful.
>
> Take a half day off to spend time with someone you care about, and remember to forget about work for those four hours!
>
> Take a vacation – Wow! There is a unique thought. You could even try it without your computer and cell phone along. I dare you!
>
> Keep an inspiring book handy and take a few minutes to read a thought several times a day. It is even better if you spend a couple more minutes contemplating the idea(s) you just read. Then send it to someone, with a kind note. [How about that difficult person? A good way to pay them attention at the same time!]

Do something positive for someone else. It is great for stress.

Call someone just because – your wife, significant other, kid, an old friend

Get some exercise – it can help energize you in the middle of the day.

Time Management

Make the choice to take a difference by accepting responsibility for your time concerns. Then make a difference by changing things and sticking to the changes. Remember: the tendency is to just add more work – don't! Add some relaxation and even fun, too. [See my book, *Leaders Managing Change*, Chapter 19, *Time Management*.]

Here is one great suggestion from my Time Management seminars:

> **Use "Little blocks of time."** We all have them – standing in lines; walking from A to B (between meetings); sitting in a car, on a plane, in a bus; during coffee breaks; five minutes in the morning; or just before you go to bed; and so on. Watch your day and you will find them; typically, lots of them.
>
> **Then use these in positive ways for yourself!** Meditation, a quick call to your wife/children, a quick stop to say "Hi" to a colleague, a moment for those deep breaths, and so on.
>
> **Note:** this is how I did a good bit of the studying for my Doctoral exams. I used my little blocks of time wisely.

Know your Limits

There are times when we have to take a step back and force ourselves to take a break. It might be just a few moments to regain composure or an actual vacation to get away. Pushing yourself past what you can <u>comfortably</u> put up with makes for a whole host of problems, especially when working with difficult behavior concerns. Not the least of which is you may become a more difficult person to work and live with yourself. If you doubt this, ask someone the next time you are 'stressed out.'

Take Care of...

> The physical You
>
> The intellectual/mental You
>
> The psychological You
>
> The spiritual You

Be able to and willing to say, "NO!"

> Hint: It is your choice, not theirs.

Celebrate what is Right with YOUR Life...
by focusing on the good stuff.

The bad stuff will demand enough of your attention as it is. This is a choice we make many times a day. Find ways in which you can enjoy all of the moments you can.

Big Hint: Making someone else's day by paying attention to them and helping take care of them is one of the best ways to celebrate what is right with your life, too.

Find your WOWS!

I can name a dozen WOWS in my life without thinking very hard – related to both my work and my life.

So can you. Spend a little time each day enjoying the great things about your work and life, and, guess what? You will be spending less time worrying, stressing, judging.

Smile

And find things every day to smile about. They are there and you don't even have to look hard, but you do have to pay attention.

Be kind to yourself

Always be kind to yourself. It helps your own growth and **it helps you in your interactions with others. The better you treat yourself the better you will treat others.** Find ways every day to treat yourself well.

Treat Yourself

Take time to treat yourself once in a while. Take time to treat yourself in small ways, every day.

- Have some dessert once a week
- Buy yourself a present
- Go shopping or go to a movie you want to see
- Spend time 'you can't afford' with a loved one without any guilt
- Buy yourself flowers or a new tool

Take care of YOU – you are worth it.

Questions and Ideas for Contemplation

You are, you know.

Chapter 25

Stay the Course

Change is not easy

Change is not easy even when we are motivated to change. We have to pay attention, work at it on a daily basis, and even practice our new skills. But it really is worth it. Our work life can become so much better when we do.

There is a lot of good material contained in this book. It pays to go back and read personally relevant sections and to take notes on things that seem important to your concerns. It is very important to **renew yourself** on a regular basis when you are doing this type of self-help work. That means re-re-reading materials that are helpful, practicing exercises or ideas that are useful, and so on.

I highly recommend acquiring other materials (There is an extensive bibliography at the end of this book.) and looking through other difficultpeople.org books available on line. All of my books will be available in Revised Second Editions within the next year. Check on line at Amazon.com, using my name in the search – Joseph E. Koob II.

Learning is on-going

I still personally work every day on areas that I know I need further work in. For me life's experiences can teach me a great deal if I pay attention and stay open to the possibilities. I can also facilitate my education by focusing on the right things myself.

Remember

Everything you do within the purview of others affects them;

it also affects you!

Choose wisely.

I sincerely hope these materials have proven useful and help you make a positive difference in your life. I know that they work because I have far fewer difficult people to deal with in my life these days

Or, is it that I know how to deal with them better?

Or, just maybe, I don't see them as difficult anymore.

Best wishes,

Joe Koob

Bibliographies

Difficult People Books by Dr. Joseph Koob

Annotated Bibliography

Understanding and Working with Difficult People

We believe this book presents the most comprehensive material available about being successful with difficult people. This book is designed to be a practical, accessible introduction to the very broad topic of dealing with difficult people/difficult behaviors. Since every difficult situation is different, the focus here will be on building a basic understanding of how you interact with difficult people, what makes difficult people tick, and the most fundamental skills you can bring to the table to help change these encounters for the better.

ME! A Difficult Person?

This is second of our signature books. This book focuses on learning more about yourself. Most of us are occasionally difficult or seen as difficult by others. This may simply be a matter of different perspectives, or it may mean that we have some inner work to do. This course is concerned with understanding more about how you come across to others, and understanding more about who you are as a person. It is also concerned with self-improvement – making changes that will help make your interactions with others significantly better, and that will bring you more peace, comfort, and joy in your life.

Difficult Spouses? Improving and Saving Your Relationship with Your Significant Other

Are you having difficulties in your current relationship? Facing a divorce? Newly divorced and trying to understand what happened and what you could have done about it? We feel this book has value not only for couples who are simply having difficulties in their relationships with their significant others, but also those facing divorce, recently divorced couples, and for people entering new relationships. The focus is on developing the knowledge, skills, and tools to help your relationship be successful.

Dealing with Difficult Strangers

Being successful in difficult situations with strangers is all about what you can bring to the situation. You will find a tremendous amount of useful information and skills included in this book that can make a significant difference in how you approach difficult strangers, how you feel as a result of these difficult encounters, and how you can emerge without a negative experience having ruined your day.

Succeeding with Difficult Professors (and Tough Courses)

A course for college students at all levels. What you need to know to make the most of your college career. This course has two main sections: "Getting along with Difficult Professors," and "Succeeding in Tough Classes." The first section will discuss ideas and skills you can use to get through personal difficulties with professors. The second section will focus on techniques, study skills, and approaches that will help you get the grades you want.

Guiding Children

Guiding and working with children is on the mind of every parent. This book focuses on skills and tools to help you as a parent provide the best possible environment for your child's development by avoiding difficulties through intelligent upbringing. This book is not only about helping you to guide your children through concerns that arise, but it is even more about enjoying your children. They do grow up, much faster than we expect. Take advantage of the tremendous joy they can bring into your life and the vast understanding of life that they provide. You will be glad you did.

Dealing with Difficult Customers

(for Employees, Companies, and Customer Service Personnel)

This book is all about putting the gamut of customer relations into a perspective that is workable, and supports you, the customer contact person, throughout.

While many businesses do provide extensive customer relations training, the focus is often fairly one way – aimed at keeping business. This book presents extensive insight and knowledge about the customer's perspective, what you need to know as a representative to fulfill your job, the internal and external support you need, and the tools and skills to communicate effectively with difficult customers.

Caring for Difficult Patients: A Guide for Nursing Professionals

I believe that the Nursing profession is one of the most admired in America. We think of Nurses as professional: that is, they have a knowledge base and skill set that is unique and valued – the quality of their work is important to them; and we think of Nurses as people who care about their patients – they are concerned with our well-being when we are under their care. These considerations are the focal point for discussing how to best deal with difficult patients

Trilogy: Dealing with Change

Books centered on Leaders working through change:

Difficult Situations - Dealing with Change

Change and difficult situations can certainly produce a great deal of angst, and as a result, difficult people. This book focuses on learning the skills and tools you need to deal with the ongoing stresses of constant change in the business world. It is about knowledgeable leadership: how what you do helps you get through change, and helps you lead others through change. It presumes you are already inspired, good, intelligent, and practical. This book is about making a difference.

Honoring Work and Life: 99 Words for Leaders to Live By

This book provides a foundation of key ideas that focus on Leadership and Personal qualities, attributes, and behaviors that honor not only our work but our life. It is my firm belief that true leaders work to serve their fellow employees, their team, their company, their customers, as well as their families and friends. This is about working on those attributes that make great leaders.

Leaders Managing Change

Leaders Managing Change is about understanding and dealing with the ongoing stresses of constant change in the business world, most importantly it is about leadership. When I thought about the concerns that are a regular part of high turnover rates, leadership changes, acquisitions and mergers, and the myriad of other transitions businesses face today, the focus came down to leadership. Good leaders get things done. This book focuses on knowledgeable leadership (i.e. what you need to know to help you deal with change as a leader). It presumes you are already inspired, good, intelligent, and practical. It is about making a difference.

Business Trilogy

Dealing with Difficult Coworkers

The emphasis here is on helping people solve the difficulties they have at work with someone who is relatively speaking a 'coworker,' or 'colleague,' in other words, someone whose 'rank' or 'job' is roughly on the same level as yours. Are you perturbed, exasperated, frustrated, angry, upset, and genuinely peeved with someone at work? We have all had occasion to work with someone who seems to have a wide range of concerns with other people in the workplace. Can we succeed with them and turn a difficult situation around? Can we enjoy our work-life once again? Definitely! This book provides you with key ideas, skills, and tools that you can use to be successful with difficult colleagues. The power is in your own inner strength and the knowledge and understanding you develop.

Succeeding with Difficult Bosses

Have a tough boss? This is a practical, in-the-trenches approach to succeeding with a difficult authority figure – a (how to) book for one of your most important relationships at work. This book is focused on understanding the unique relationship we have with a person who has hierarchical power over us. To truly gain the knowledge we need to be successful with difficult bosses, we need to understand who they are as a person and what they do that frustrates us. We must also understand ourselves – how we subconsciously add to the mix, and how we can change our outlook and behavior so that our boss will change his/her behavior in relationship to us. When people talk about difficult bosses, the root of their concerns is often that they FEEL unappreciated, put down, 'less than,' i.e., treated almost as a non-entity. If you feel this way, this book was written for you

Managing Difficult Employees

This book is about what YOU as a manager and leader bring to the table. It addresses two key questions: Is your leadership conducive to a positive work environment with few personnel concerns; and, when concerns do arise, are you prepared to handle them effectively and efficiently? The first part of this book focuses on avoiding difficulties through knowledgeable and inspired leadership. Part II of this work will demonstrate how to apply your personal strengths and your management and leadership skills to working successfully with difficult personnel concerns and in difficult situations.

A Perfect Day: Guide for a Better Life

Dr. Koob's award-winning book about working toward your own personal perfect day – Best Book Non-fiction, 1999, Oklahoma Writer's Federation; Merit award 2000, Writer's Digest. [Paperback available at major on-line retailers]

Difficult People Materials

Axelrod, A and Holtje, J., *201 Ways to Deal with Difficult People*, McGraw-Hill, New York, 1997.

Bell, A. and Smith, D., *Winning with Difficult People*, Barron's, New York, 1997

Bramson, Robert M., *Coping with Difficult Bosses*, Fireside, New York, 1992.

Bramson, Robert M., *Coping with Difficult People*, Anchor Press, New York, 1981.

Braunstein, Barbara, *How to Deal with Difficult People*, Skillpath Publications, Mission, KS, 1994. [Tapes]

Brinkman, R. and Kirschner, R., *Dealing with People You Can't Stand,* McGraw-Hill, New York, 1994.

Carter, Jay, *Nasty Bosses: How to STOP BEING HURT by them without stooping to THEIR level*, McGraw-Hill, New York, 2004.

Case, Gary and Rhoades-Baum, *How to Handle Difficult Customers*, Help Deck Institute, Colorado Springs, 1994.

Cava, Roberta, *Dealing with Difficult People: How to Deal with Nasty Customers, Demanding Bosses and Annoying Co-workers*, Firefly Books, Buffalo, NY, 2004.

Cava, Roberta, *difficult people: How to Deal with Impossible clients, Bosses, and Employees*, Firefly Books, Buffalo, NY, 1990.

Cavaiola, A. And Lavender, N., *Toxic Coworkers: How to Deal with Dysfunctional People on the Job*, New Harbinger Publications, Oakland, CA, 2000.

Costello, Andrew, *How to Deal with Difficult People*, Ligori Publications, Liguri, MI, 1980.

Crowe, Sandra, *Since Strangling Isn't An Option*, Perigee, New York, 1999.

Diehm, William, *How to Get Along with Difficult People*, Broadman Press, Nashville, 1992.

Felder, Leonard, *Does Someone Treat You Badly? How to Handle Brutal Bosses, Crazy Coworkers...and Anyone Else Who Drives You Nuts*, Berkley Books, NY, 1993.

First, Michael, Ed., *Diagnostic and Statistical Manual for Mental Disorders*, 4th Edition, American Psychiatric Asso.,Washington, 1994.

Friedman, Paul, *How to Deal with Difficult People*, SkillPath Publications, Mission, KS, 1994.

Gill, Lucy, *How to Work with Just About Anyone*, Fireside, New York, 1999.

Griswold, Bob, *Coping with Difficult and Negative People and Personal Magnetism*, Effective Learning Systems, Inc., Edina, MN. [Tape]

Holloway, Andy, "Bad Boss Blues," *Canadian Business*, 24 Oct 2004.

Hoover, John, *How to Work for an Idiot: Survive & Thrive Without Killing Your Boss*, Career Press, Princeton, NJ, 2004.

Jones, Katina, *Succeeding with Difficult People*, Longmeadow Press, Stamford, CT, 1992.

Keating, Charles, *Dealing with Difficult People*, Paulist Press, New York, 1984.

Littauer, Florence, *How to Get Along with Difficult People*, Harvest House, Eugene, 1984.

Lloyd, Ken, *Jerks at Work: How to Deal with People Problems and Problem People*, Career Press, Franklin Lakes, NJ, 1999

Lundin, W. and Lundin, J., *When Smart People Work for Dumb Bosses: How to Survive in a Crazy and Dysfunctional Workplace*, McGraw-Hill, New York, 1998.

Markham, Ursula, *How to deal with Difficult people*, Thorsons, London, 1993.

Meier, Paul, *Don't Let Jerks Get the Best of You: Advice for Dealing with Difficult People*, Thomas Nelson, Nashville, 1993.

Namie, G. and Namie, R., *the Bully at Work*, Sourcebooks, Inc., Naperville, IL, 2000.

Osbourne, Christina, *Dealing with Difficult People*, DK, London, 2002.

Oxman, Murray, *The How to Easily Handle Difficult People, Success Without Stress*, Morro Bay, CA, 1997.

Perkins, Betty, *Lion Taming: The Courage to Deal with Difficult People Including Yourself*, Tzedakah Publications, Scramento, 1995.

Rosen, Mark, *Thank You for Being Such A Pain: Spiritual Guidance for Dealing with Difficult People*, Three Rivers Press, New York, 1998.

Segal, Judith, *Getting Them to See It Your Way: Dealing with Difficult and Challenging People*, Lowell House, Los Angeles, 2000.

Solomon, Muriel, *Working with Difficult People*, Prentice Hall, Englewood Cliffs,1990.

Toropov, Brandon, *The Complete Idiot's Guide to Getting Along with Difficult People*, Alpha Books, New York, 1997.

Toropov, Brandon, *Manager's Guide to Dealing with Difficult People*, Prentice Hall, Paramus, NJ, 1997.

Turecki, Stanley, *The Difficult Child*, Bantam Books, NY, 1989.

Weiner, David L., *Power Freaks: Dealing with Them in the Workplace or Anywhere*, Prometheus Books, Amherst, New York, 2002

Weiss, Donald, *How to Deal with Difficult People*, Amacon, New York, 1987.

Recommended Readings

Dewey, John, *Democracy and Education*, Norwood Press, Norwood, MA, 1916.

Dewey, John, *Education and Experience*, Kappa Delta Pi Publications, Macmillian, New York, 1938.

Dyer, Wayne, *Pulling Your Own Stri*ngs, Funk and Wagnalls, New York, 1978.

Dyer, Wayne, *Your Erroneous Zones*, Funk and Wagnalls, New York, 1976.

Dyer, Wayne, *Your Sacred Self*, Harper, New York, 1995.

Guraik, David B., Editor, *Webster's New World Dictionary*, World Publishing, New York, 1972.

Heinlein, Robert, *Time Enough for Love*, New English Library, New York, 1974.

Hesse, Hermann, *Narcissus and Goldmund*, Bantam, New York, 1971.

James, M, and Jongeward, D. *Born to Win*, Addison-Wesley, 1971.

Koob, Joseph, *A Perfect Day: Guide for A Better Life*, NEJS Publications, Lawton, OK, 1998.

Parrott, Thomas Marc, Ed., *Shakespeare: Twenty-three Plays and the Sonnets*, Charles Scribner's Sons, Washington, D.C., 1938.

Pirsig, Robert, *Zen and the Art of Motorcycle Maintenance*, Bantam, New York, 1980.

Rand, Ayn, *Atlas Shrugged*, Signet Books, New York, 1957.

Redman, Ben Ray, Editor, *The Portable Voltaire*, Viking Press, New York, 1949.

Change and Leadership

Bolles, Richard N., *What Color is Your Parachute?* Ten Speed Press, Berkeley, CA, 1987.

Bridges, William, *Managing Transitions: Making the Most of Change*, Perseus Books, Cambridge, 1991.

Bridges, William, *Transitions: Making Sense of Life's Changes*, Perseus Books, Cambridge, 1980.

Buckingham, Marcus, & Coffman, Curt, *First, Break All the Rules: What the World's Greatest Managers Do Differently*, Simon and Schuster, New York, 1999.

Collins, J., and Porras, J., *Built to Last: Successful Habits of Visionary Companies*, Harper Business, NY, 2001.

Collins, Jim, *Good TO Great: Why Some Companies Make the Leap...and Others Don't*, Harper Business, NY, 2001.

Cooper, Robert and Sawaf, Ayman, *Executive EQ: Emotional Intelligence in Leadership & Organizations*, Grisset/Putnam, New York, 1996.

Crane, Thomas, *The Heart of Coaching*, FTA Press, San Diego, 1998.

Deits, Bob, Life *After Loss: A Personal Guide Dealing with Death, Divorce, Job Change and Relocation*, Fisher Books, Tucson, 1988.

Dominhguez, Linda R., *How to Shine at Work*, McGraw Hill, 2003.

Drucker, Peter F., *Managing in a Time of Great Change*, Truman Talley Books, NY, 1995.

Evard, Beth L. And Gipple, Craig A., *Managing Business Change for Dummies*, Hungry Minds, Inc., NY,2001.

Farson, Richard and Keyes, Ralph, *Whoever Makes the Most Mistakes Wins: The Paradox of Innovation*, Free Press, NY, 2002.

Fortgang, Laura Berman, *Take Yourself to the Top: The Secrets of America's #1 Career Coach*, Warner Books, New York, 1998.

Gates, Bill, *Business " the Speed of Thought: Succeeding in the Digital Economy*, Warner Books, New York, 1999.

Gerstner, Jr., Louis, V, *Who Says Elephants Can't Dance? Leading a Great Enterprise Through Dramatic Change*, HarperBusiness, New York, 2002.

Going Through Bereavement–When a loved one dies, Langeland Memorial Chapel, Kalamazoo, MI.

Grieve, Bradly T., *The Blue Day Book: A Lesson in Cheering Yourself Up*, Andrews McMeel Publishing, Kansas City, 2000.

Goldratt, Eliyahu M., *Critical Chain*, North River Press, Great Barrington, MA, 1997.

Hammer, Michael and Champy, James, *Reengineering the Corporation: A Manifesto for Business Revolution, HarperBusiness*, New York, 1993.

Hoffer, Eric, *The Ordeal of Change*, Harper & Row, NY, 1952.

Jeffreys, J. Shep. *Coping with Workplace Change: Dealing with Loss and Grief*, Crisp Productions, Menlo Park, CA, 1995.

Johnson, Spencer, *Who Moved My Cheese*, G. P. Putnam, New York, 1998.

Kanter, Rosabeth Moss, *The Change Masters: Innovation & Entrepreneurship in the American Corporation*, Simon & Schuster, New York, 1983.

Kelley, Robert, *How to be a Star at Work: Nine Breakthrough Strategies You Need to Succeed*, Random House, New York, 1998.

Koob, Joseph E. II, *Difficult Situations: Dealing with Change*, NEJS Publications, Saline, MI, 2004.

Kotter, John P, *Leading Change*, Harvard Business School Press, Boston, 1996.

Kotter, John P, *The Leadership Factor*, Free Press, New York, 1988.

Kouzes, J. and Posner, B., *Credibility: How Leaders Gain and Lose it; Why People Demand it*, Jossey-Bass Publishers, San Francisco, 1993.

Kuster, Elizabeth, *Exorcising Your Ex*, Fireside, New York, 1996.

Leonard, George, *Mastery: The Keys to Success and Long-term Fulfillment*, Plume, NY 1992.

Lunden, Joan, and Cagan, Andrea, *A Bend in the Road is Not the End of the Road*, William Morrow, New York, 1998.

Maxwell, John C., *The 21 Indispensible Qualities of Leadership: Becoming the Person Others Will Want to Follow*, Thomas Nelson Publishers, Nashville, 1999.

Maxwell, John C., *The 17 Indisputable Laws of Teamwork: Embrace them and Empower Your Team*, Thomas Nelson Publishers, Nashville, 2001.

Maxwell, John C., *21 Irrefutable Laws of Leadership*, Thomas Nelson, Inc., Nashville, 1998.

Milwid, Beth, *Working With Men: Professional Women Talk About Power, Sexuality, and Ethics*, Beyond Words, Kingsport, TN, 1990.

McKay, Harvey, *Swim with the Sharks: Without Being Eaten Alive*, William Morrow Co., New York, 1988.

Messer, Bonnie J., *Dealing with Change*, Abington Press, 1996.

Montalbo, Thomas, *The Power of Eloquence: Magic Key to Success in Public Speaking*, Prentive-Hall, Englewood Cliffs, N.J., 1984.

Pasternack, Bruce and Viscio, Albert, *The Centerless Corporation: A New Model for Transforming Your Organization for Growth and Prosperity*, Fireside, New York, 1998.

Peters, Tom, *The Circle of Innovation: You Can't Shrink Your Way to Greatnness*, Vintage Books, New York, 1999.

Peters, Tom, *Liberation Management: Necessary Disorganization for the Nanosecond Nineties*, Faucett Columbine, New York, 1992.

Peters, Tom, and Waterman, Robert, *In Search of Excellence: Lessons from America's Best-Run Companies*, Harper & Row, New York, 1982.

Peters, Tom, and Austin, Nancy, *A Passion for Excellence: The Leadership Difference*, Random House, New York, 1985.

Peters, Tom, *The Pursuit of WOW! Every Person's Guide to Topsy-Turvy Times*, Vintage Books, New York, 1994.

Peters, Tom, *Professional Service Firm 50: Fifty Ways to Transform Your "Department" into a Professional Service Firm whose Trademarks are Passion and Excellence*, Alfred A. Knopf, 1999.

Peters, Tom, *Re-imagine! Business Excellence in a Disruptive Age*, DK, London, 2003.

Peters, Tom, *Thriving on Chaos: Handbook for a Management Revolution*, Alfred Knopf, New York, 1987

Popcorn, Faith, *EVEolutuon: The Eight Truths of Marketing to Women*, Hyperion Books, 2001.

Smith, Hyrum W. The *10 Natural Laws of Successful Time and Life Management: Proven Strategies for Increased Productivity and Inner Peace*, Warner Books, New York, 1994.

Talbot, Kay, *The Ten Biggest Myths About Grief*, Abbey Press, St. Meinrad, IN, 2000.

Waterman, Robert H., Jr., *The Renewal Factor: How The Best Get And Keep The Competitive Edge*, Bantam, New York, 1986.

Whitmore, John, *Coaching for Performance*, Nicholas Brealey Publishing, London, 1999.

Printed in Great Britain
by Amazon